edges

Assessment for Learning in English

Lindsay McNab

Imelda Pilgrim

Marian Slee

Contributors: David Grant and Peter Thomas
Series consultant: Susan Sutton

3

www.heinemann.co.uk

✓ Free online support
✓ Useful weblinks
✓ 24 hour online ordering

01865 888058

Contents

If you are studying *The Tempest* instead of *Much Ado About Nothing*, you could use the alternative resources for *The Tempest* on our website – www.heinemann.co.uk

The following icons are used in this book:

 This indicates that **next steps** activities and teaching notes are available in the Assessment and Resource File 3 and Teacher's Handbook 3.

 This indicates that a supplementary activity, or worksheet to support a Student Book activity, is available in the Assessment and Resource File 3.

Introduction

The whole picture

In this book you will explore how writers write, readers read, speakers speak and listeners listen. You will develop skills in assessing your own learning and working out what you need to do to make good progress. By the end of the book we hope you will feel in control and ready to move on.

WHAT? You will:
- become a sharper and more perceptive reader and researcher
- develop your talents as a writer
- gain confidence and skill as a speaker and a listener
- take control of your own learning

HOW? by:
- reading and researching a range of lively, interesting, focused texts
- experimenting with different note-making methods, writing styles and techniques
- working with other students in formal and informal situations
- assessing your work and using the feedback and progress checks to track your learning and set your own targets

WHY? because:
- better reading and research skills help you to understand and interpret your world
- writing is an important form of communication
- increasing your confidence in speaking and listening helps you to deal effectively with different situations
- when you know what you are learning, and why you are learning it, you make better progress.

1 Media angles

The bigger picture

In this unit you will study a range of media texts including newspaper and magazine articles, radio broadcasts and information texts. You will learn how texts are put together and how they influence their audiences. You will also compare the ways ideas are presented in different texts. You will think about the ways in which writers' points of view are reflected in their writing. At the end of the unit you will produce a radio news item based on a range of information.

WHAT? You will:
- understand how presentational techniques are used
- use presentational devices to appeal to a specific audience
- analyse and explain the ways in which writers choose words
- plan, structure and write a formal essay
- evaluate the reliability of information in news stories
- analyse how media texts are influenced by readers

HOW? by:
- studying the presentational devices in a range of texts
- evaluating the presentational devices in your own texts
- comparing and analysing different kinds of texts
- exploring how news stories are put together from a range of sources

WHY? because:
- studying presentational effects will help you to use them effectively in your own writing
- writing formal essays will help you to write well in several subjects across the curriculum
- understanding how media texts influence readers helps you to develop analytical skills that you can use in a range of subjects.

Exploring media texts

'The media' is a term used to describe forms of communication that reach large numbers of people. Media texts can be visual, written or auditory (involving listening skills) and can be divided into two categories: broadcast and print. Audiences use media texts for a range of reasons:

- to be informed and educated
- to be entertained
- to use the media as a talking point with friends
- to escape from their daily lives into other worlds and situations
- to identify with characters and situations to learn more about themselves.

Activity 1

1 With a partner, make a list of media texts you are already aware of. Discuss what you think their audience and purpose are. Set out your answers in a table like the one below, and aim to include at least **five** more media texts.

Media text	Broadcast	Print	Audience	Purpose
Newspapers		✓	Mainly adults	Entertain, inform

2 Discuss with your partner which media would be the most appropriate for:

- advice on the dangers of smoking
- an advertisement for trainers
- a documentary about dolphins
- the latest news, weather and travel information.

Share your answers with another pair of students. If you have chosen different media, discuss your reasons for your choice.

3 Using the list at the top of this page, work out the reasons why people access the following:

- soap operas such as *Coronation Street*
- a horoscope
- a radio broadcast of a football match
- an advertisement for a new sports shop
- TV news.

 Highlight thinking

Establishing prior learning
It makes sense to reflect on what you already know before you begin to develop new ideas. Taking time to think about and note down your prior learning or existing knowledge will help you to:

- establish how much you already know/understand
- create a foundation for new learning
- identify areas of strength and gaps.

Examining magazines

Every magazine has:
- **a purpose** – the reason why it was written
- **an audience** – the people who read the magazine.

Activity 2

With a partner, write down the names of magazines you know and suggest reasons why people buy them. You can use the list at the top of page 6 to help you answer this question.

When thinking about a magazine's audience you should consider age, gender, interests and lifestyle. In order to make money it is important that the magazine publishers attract their target audience. They do this by including items and advertising products that will be of particular interest to their readers and by presenting the magazine in ways that will appeal to them.

Magazines can be divided into categories according to their subject matter.
- **General interest magazines** cover a wide range of topics and interests.
- **Special interest magazines** are written to appeal to readers with particular interests such as fishing or football. For example: *Mountain Biking* is targeted at people who are keen on this particular sport.

Activity 3

With a partner, look at the magazine covers on the next page. Decide on the audience, purpose and type (general interest or specialist) of each one. Show your answers as spider diagrams, like this:

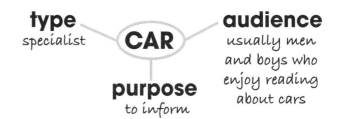

For each magazine, explain how the writers have included features aimed specifically at their target audience.

Activity 4

Tell a partner about a magazine you are familiar with. You should comment on:

- its target audience
- its content (articles, interviews, etc.) and how this appeals to readers
- its appearance (design and layout)
- reasons why the target audience would enjoy reading this magazine.

Comparing presentational devices on magazine covers

First impressions and visual impact are very important. To attract attention and to encourage people to buy the magazine, designers make their covers as eye-catching as possible. When assessing a front cover you should think about how each of the following is intended to have an effect on readers:

- first impressions
- use of colour
- illustrations
- use of headlines
- use of fonts
- use of punctuation
- layout
- use of words.

Activity 5

Look closely at the magazine covers on pages 10–11. What is the intended audience for each magazine? Which category does each one fall into – general interest or specialist? To help you compare the covers, answer the questions that follow as you study each cover. Set out your notes in a table like the one below.

	Text A	Text B
Title		
Use of colour		

Title
- What is the title?
- What associations does it suggest?

Use of colour
- What are the main colours on the cover?
- What effect do these colours create for readers?
- How are background colour and lighting used to create a particular effect?

Illustrations
- What is the topic of the main picture?
- How have the designers chosen to present the central image?
- How is this image used to attract readers?

Layout
- What slogans appear underneath the main picture?
- How do these slogans make a link with the picture?
- What effect are the slogans meant to have on readers?
- How have the sub-headings been made appropriate for the target audience?
- How do the sub-headings attract readers to the magazine?

Use of fonts
- How many different fonts can you see on the cover?
- Why have the designers used different fonts?
- How do the different styles reflect the interests of the readers?

Targeting readers
- Write two sentences to summarise the impression each cover gives to readers and to explain how it captures the interest of the target audience.

🔖 Sharpen punctuation

Using a range of punctuation

The magazine covers on pages 10–11 use a similar range of punctuation. Can you explain why each of the following is used and what effect it is intended to have on the reader? Support your explanations with examples from the covers.

1 Exclamation marks
2 Question marks
3 Speech marks

How does the punctuation affect the way readers respond to the texts?

Text A

Text B

Comparing on-line and print magazines

So far, you have examined magazines aimed at different audiences. You will have found differences in their presentation, but also similarities, as they are both printed magazines.

The text below is the home page of an on-line magazine (one that appears on the Internet). You will notice that it differs in some ways from the print magazine covers.

Activity 6

1 With a partner, list the similarities and differences between the presentational devices used in on-line and print magazines. Set out your answers in a table like the one below.

Presentational device	On-line magazine	Print magazines	Similar	Different
Title	Small font, does not stand out	Large font, stands out		✗
Use of colour				
Illustrations				
Layout				
Fonts				
Headings and sub-headings				

2 a Who do you think is the audience for this on-line magazine? How is this different from the magazines you have studied so far?

b What are the advantages of an on-line magazine compared with a print magazine?

c What are the disadvantages of an on-line magazine compared with a print magazine?

d Why are there differences in presentation between the two types of magazine?

e Can you explain the similarities between them?

 Feedback

Compare your answers with a partner's. Has either of you included points that the other has not? Amend your answers to include any additional points that you have discussed with your partner.

Analysing the language and content of magazine covers

So far, you have looked at the presentation of magazine covers. Now you are going to examine other ways in which magazine covers appeal to readers through their choice of language and content. The following activities will help to prepare you to write a formal essay entitled:
Analyse the ways in which the designers of magazine covers aim to influence their readers.

Activity 7

1 Copy out the table below. For each type of content, find an example from **at least one** of the magazines you have studied so far in this unit.

Content	Magazine	Topic
True-life stories	*Sugar* *BBC Teens*	'My boyfriend got me hooked on heroin' 'Living with parents who use drugs'
Games		
Quizzes		
Campaigns		
Lifestyle/advice		
Beauty/personal appearance		
Others		

2 Are there any topics that the magazines have in common?

3 Do you think the magazine writers have selected topics that will appeal to teenagers?

4 Suggest reasons why *BBC Teens* magazine has separate boys' and girls' sections.

5 Find **two** differences between the boys' and girls' sections.

Non-standard English

To appeal to their audience, writers use language that their readers will relate to. If the magazine covers were written entirely in standard English they would be less appealing to teenagers.

Non-standard English contains words and expressions that are not necessarily understood by everyone. For example, the sentence: 'Done anything embarrassing lately? Then spill your stories on the Cringewall' (non-standard English) could be written as: 'Have you done anything embarrassing lately? If so, share your stories on the Cringewall' (standard English), but might not have the same appeal to teenagers.

Activity 8

Try this out for yourself by rewriting the following in standard English.
- It's just not cool.
- Zap those prob zits once and for all.
- The ultimate babe magnet.

Activity 9

Look at the *Sugar*, *PowerStation* and *BBC Teens* covers (pages10–12).

1 Write down examples of non-standard English from each magazine.

2 Write down examples of the writers addressing their readers directly. What effect does this have on readers?

3 Why is it important for magazine writers to use the same language as their readers?

4 Magazine writers sometimes influence their audience by using language that appeals to their emotions. For example, in the phrase 'Secrets revealed!' (*PowerStation*, page 11) the word 'revealed' suggests readers will enjoy discovering something that many people may not know.

Find **one** example from each of the magazines where writers use language to appeal to their readers' emotions. Explain what emotion each one appeals to.

Writing a formal essay

Sometimes you are asked to analyse texts in a formal essay. Essays need to be carefully structured. Explore the features of formal essay writing on the following page. You will notice the entire essay is written in formal standard English.

Analyse the ways in which the designers of the video advertisement have influenced their audience.

1 Short introduction linking directly with wording of task.

The designers of the advertisement set out to influence their audience in a variety of ways.

2 Connective used to order ideas. Find four more connectives signalling further points.

First, they have used very bright bold colours for the background so that this will catch the reader's eye instantly. In addition, the title of the video is in bright yellow lettering and is placed in the centre of the page so that it will be noticed easily. They have also used the main characters from the video in the centre of the page.

3 Phrase introducing analysis. Find another phrase used to introduce analysis.

In this way they give the reader some idea of what to expect in the video. The girl on the left looks very determined and slightly menacing, as if to suggest that there will be some kind of struggle. This will influence audiences who enjoy action films.

4 Example from the text. Find one other example.

The central characters are surrounded by smaller figures who are also in the film. There are lot of these figures which give the advert a busy energetic appearance. As a result this will appeal to young people who like lively action-packed videos.

The slogan at the top of the advertisement 'Breaking out of prison was never this much fun' appeals to readers by creating a sense of excitement. The word 'fun' convinces readers that they will enjoy this film. The word 'fun' has greater impact because an exclamation mark is placed at the end of it for emphasis and the use of ellipsis before the word creates a slight pause and builds up some tension. When the writers say 'From the producers of "Ghost in the Shell"' they are creating an association with another film the readers might know and like, thus influencing them to buy the video of 'Dead Leaves'.

5 Selection of textual detail analysed closely to explain the effect on the reader. Find another place where the effect on the reader is explained.

Overall this advertisement has a dynamic energetic feel and would definitely influence young people and encourage them to buy or rent the video.

6 Short conclusion to sum up ideas, refers back to title of task.

Activity 10

Using the model essay on page 16 as a guide, write your own formal essay entitled: **Analyse the ways in which the designers of magazine covers set out to influence their readers**.

> ### Success criteria
>
> ☆ Refer to a range of different aspects from the magazine covers, including:
>   - use of colour and images
>   - fonts
>   - headings and layout
>   - use of language and punctuation.
> ☆ Use examples from each of the magazines to analyse the effects on readers.
> ☆ Use the **P**oint, **E**vidence, **E**xplanation model to analyse the effect on readers.
> ☆ Introduce your comments with phrases such as *in this way*, *for this reason*.
> ☆ Link your ideas using connectives such as *first*, *in addition*, *also*.

Step 1

Plan your work by deciding:
- the order in which you will analyse the use of colour, images, layout, contents, language and punctuation
- which examples you will use to support your points.

Step 2

Write your first draft. Remember your task is to **analyse** how readers are influenced. When you examine examples in detail, follow the pattern:
Point + **E**vidence + **E**xplanation of effect, for example:

point   evidence

girls relate to true-life stories such as 'Dolphins saved my life'.
The word 'my' suggests the story will be a personal account, helping explanation
readers to understand that this is a personal experience and possibly one of effect
they could relate to. This will influence them to buy the magazine.

Step 3

Check your work against the success criteria at the start of the activity.
Add anything you have left out.

 **Feedback**

Swap your work with a partner and tick each other's work in the places where you have met the success criteria. Ask your partner to help you add anything you may have missed out. Make any changes or additions you feel are necessary before you write the final draft.

✓ Progress check

Draw a ladder with five rungs. Copy the success criteria onto the rungs, with the easiest at the bottom and the most difficult at the top.

Draw a star next to the rung you feel you reached in your essay. Explain what you found difficult about reaching the next rung.

If you have already reached the top of the ladder, explain why the criterion on the top rung was the most challenging.

Presenting information

Presentational devices are used to attract readers to information texts, just as they are used on the covers of magazines. With a partner, list the different types of information text you are familiar with. Look closely at the text on page 19, then complete the activity below.

Activity 11

1 Make a list of the presentational devices in the text on page 19. You may find it helpful to look back at page 17 to remind yourself what these are.

2 Select **three** presentational devices you think work well in this text. Explain why each has been used and its intended effect.

3 Suggest **three** reasons why presentational devices are important in an information text like the one on page 19.

4 This text is written in a formal style. Find and write down **five** examples of formal vocabulary – either single words or phrases.
Compare your answers with a partner's. Did they choose the same words as you? If not, add their words to your list.

5 Who do you think is the audience for this text? Give reasons.

6 Although this is an information text, it also attempts to influence readers: the study centre is presented in a positive way. Find and write down **four** examples of words and phrases that give a positive image.

Activity 12

Rewrite and re-present the information from the information leaflet. Your audience will be young people aged 14–16. Read the success criteria on page 20 and then follow Steps 1–4.

Success criteria

☆ Inclusion of appropriate information about opportunities at the study centre.
☆ Use of language that will appeal to young people.
☆ Addressing the reader directly.
☆ Use of presentational devices such as colour, range of fonts, eye-catching headings and sub-headings in an eye-catching layout.
☆ Use of punctuation to engage the reader.

Step 1
List the information you think young people need to know. You do not have to include all of the information in the original text.

Step 2
Write out the text for your information leaflet. Aim to give a positive picture of the study centre by selecting words and phrases that will appeal to your readers.

Step 3
Design the layout for your leaflet, planning where you will use presentational devices. Decide where you will place your text.

Step 4
Write out the final version of your text, incorporating all of your presentational devices.

 Sharpen spelling

Word families
A word family is a group of words that share the same root, for example:
eight – eighty – eightieth
permanent – permanently – permanence

If you learn to spell several words in the same word family you will increase your spelling power. Use a dictionary to find and write down the word families of the words below.

innovative   **inspire**
create   **motivate**

Underline the part of the word that remains the same as the original word (the root).

Feedback

1 Swap texts with another student and award each other one, two or three stars following the system below.

⭐ Some successful features, but more work needed in a few places.

⭐⭐ A range of successful features, but more work needed on one or two.

⭐⭐⭐ Includes all the features from the success criteria list.

2 Ask your partner to explain where you could improve your work.
3 Write comments on your work explaining:
   • what features you are pleased with   • where you could improve it.

Bias and objectivity in the media

You are now going to explore a different range of media texts. The activities in this section will focus on news stories. News stories can be found in a range of media: newspapers, the Internet, radio and television are the most obvious ones. News stories contain a mixture of **facts** and **opinions**. Facts can be checked and proved: *it is raining* is a fact. An opinion is a statement of a point of view: *the weather is not very nice today* is an opinion.

A writer's choice of words can be objective or biased. *The dog bit the police officer* is objective, whereas *The vicious dog savaged the helpless police officer* is a biased way of writing the same thing.

Activity 13

The two texts on pages 22–3 are about the same topic. Read them and complete the questions below.

1 Look at these phrases from text A and decide how factual or biased they are:
   - animal-rights extremists
   - wreaked havoc in the stables
   - two beagle puppies.

2 The master of the VAGSB is quoted in Text A as saying that the intruders' intention was 'to cause havoc'. Does the writer of the article share this opinion? What evidence do you have for this?

3 Text A appeared on a website. Decide which of these websites it appeared on and explain how you know:
   - one run by an organisation that dislikes hunting with hounds
   - one run by an organisation that supports hunting with hounds
   - a news organisation that supports neither of the two points of view expressed above.

4 List the facts that appear in the story in Text B. Is the writer being objective or biased? Explain your answer.

5 Write down three words that are used in Text B to describe pro-hunters and show that the writer has a poor opinion of them. Next to each one, write what it tells you about the writer's opinion and why. For example:

Rowdy – this word is used to describe the demonstration. It is used to create an unfavourable response to the crowd, suggesting that people were loud and unpleasant.

Text A

Beagle puppies stolen from hunt kennels

The Vale of Aylesbury with Garth and South Berks Hunt (VAGSB) was last night the target of animal-rights extremists, who stole two beagle puppies and wreaked havoc in the stables.

Intruders broke into the VAGSB hunt kennels on the night of 27th October. As well as breaking into and ransacking the feed store, the perpetrators stole two beagle puppies from the kennels. The puppies, who are ear-tagged and from the Old Berkeley Beagles, were being looked after by a member of the VAGSB staff.

Alan Hill, master of the VAGSB, said: 'We have an idea who did this. The main thing is to ensure that the beagle pups are returned safely – their well-being is obviously our prime concern. However, they are tattooed, so we would hope for their swift return.

'The tack room was untouched, and the burglar alarm wasn't activated, so we are absolutely certain that the motive of the intruders was simply to cause havoc.'

Text B

League deplores hunt harassment in Brighton

According to the League Against Cruel Sports, the rowdy demonstration by the Countryside Alliance at the Labour Party conference in Brighton today reveals yet again the ugly face of the hunting fraternity. As pro-hunt **extremists** let off firecrackers and harassed conference delegates with abuse, the Police arrested two men for dumping animal carcasses. The remains of two calves and a horse were found in Brighton, to the shock and disgust of local passers-by.

Douglas Batchelor, Chief Executive of the League Against Cruel Sports, commented: 'Despite the Countryside Alliance's attempts to distance themselves from the violence consistently **perpetrated** by their members, it is clear that CA demonstrations, as we witnessed in Parliament Square and in Exeter, are far from peaceful.

'These bully-boy tactics are **counterproductive**, will alienate the general public, and lose the little support these people are clinging on to.

'It is arrogant of the pro-hunting extremists to assume that they can overthrow the will of the democratically elected House of Commons and 76 per cent of the public who want to see an end to hunting with dogs.'

This comes in the wake of threats of **intimidation** against numerous MPs such as Alun Michael MP, Minister for Rural Affairs, Candy Atherton MP, and Tony Banks MP. League campaigners and supporters the length and breadth of the country have also reported an increase in threatening and intimidating behaviour from hunters.

Word bank

extremists people who hold views that are very different from most people's and who do outrageous things
perpetrated carried out
counterproductive will not achieve the desired effect
intimidation bullying/terror

 Sharpen spelling

Learning difficult spellings

One way is to use a **mnemonic** – a trick to help you learn something. It might be a saying such as *There's a rat in 'separate'*.

Alternatively, some people break long words down into separate syllables: many people say *Wed-nes-day* inside their head when they are writing *Wednesday*.

Think about methods that might help people to learn the following words from Text B.
perpetrated **campaigners** **intimidation**

Write down a method that might help you and others to remember how to spell these words.

Changing the writer's stance

A writer's stance is his or her point of view. Texts A and B (pages 22–3) come from websites of opposing groups concerned with the issue of hunting with hounds. It would be possible to rewrite each story in a way that changes the writer's stance, for example Text A:

> The Vale of Aylesbury with Garth and South Berks Hunt (VAGSB) was last night the target of animal-rights extremists, who stole two beagle puppies and wreaked havoc in the stables.

could be changed to:

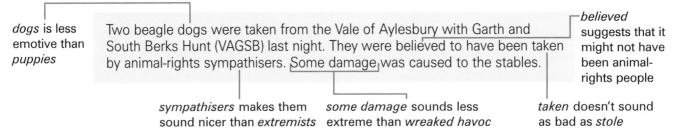

dogs is less emotive than *puppies*

Two beagle dogs were taken from the Vale of Aylesbury with Garth and South Berks Hunt (VAGSB) last night. They were believed to have been taken by animal-rights sympathisers. Some damage was caused to the stables.

believed suggests that it might not have been animal-rights people

sympathisers makes them sound nicer than *extremists*

some damage sounds less extreme than *wreaked havoc*

taken doesn't sound as bad as *stole*

Activity 14

Look at the details in the first paragraph of Text B. Change the following phrases to make them:

a more objective

b even more biased.

- the rowdy demonstration
- pro-hunt extremists
- harassed conference delegates with abuse.

Feedback

Read your suggested changes to a partner. When you have both read and listened to each other's choices of words, decide between you which phrases would lead to:

a the most objective account

b the most biased account.

Evaluating information

The same material may be shaped in different ways for the media to present a news story with a different slant.

The news story on page 25 has been put together by a writer who wants to include some facts about an event and opinions that reflect the opposing points of view about hunting.

Activity 15

1 Read the seven paragraphs of the article below and decide whether each one is:

  a mainly factual

  b mainly the opinions of pro-hunters

  c mainly the opinions of anti-hunters.

Copy the table below and write a, b, or c under each paragraph number.

Para 1	Para 2	Para 3	Para 4	Para 5	Para 6	Para 7

2 How would you rate the objectivity of this article on a scale of 1–5, where 1 = strongly biased towards the pro-hunters and 5 = strongly biased towards the anti-hunters? In deciding, think about the following:

- the amount of space devoted to each side
- where in the article the writer places the opinions of each side
- the headline.

When you have decided, write a very brief explanation of your answer.

Hunt set for biggest day in its history

22 December 2003

1 Fox hunters in Warwickshire are planning the biggest day of hunting in their history on Boxing Day.

2 Twenty-one West Midlands hunts will take place on 26 December and the hunters – who are issuing an open invitation to the hunts – believe thousands of supporters will also turn up at the events.

3 But the League Against Cruel Sports, which wants to see an end to hunting with dogs, has organised 21 official protests across the UK to campaign against the sport. Warwickshire's hunts have been advertising details of their meets and have been inviting the public to watch the hunt at work.

4 Countryside Alliance spokesman Clare Rowson said: 'Warwickshire's hunts are proud of their way of life and the good they do for our countryside, wildlife, communities and the rural economy.

5 'That is why they encourage people to join them, not just on Boxing Day but throughout the year, and why more people are hunting now than ever before.'

6 The Warwickshire hunt is taking place from 10.45am at Upton House in Banbury; Atherstone hunt will meet at Market Bosworth at 11am; and Warwickshire Beagles will meet at the Rose and Crown in Feckenham, Worcestershire at noon.

7 Douglas Batchelor, Chief Executive of the League Against Cruel Sports, said: 'The number of people taking part in these hunts will be vastly outnumbered by the huge number of people across the country who want to see this barbaric practice stopped. This is a final desperate show of force by a hunting community who know that legislation banning hunting will soon become a reality.'

Activity 16

A local radio station wants to use the news article on page 25 to provide **some factual information** about what is happening on Boxing Day. The station does not wish to report the opinions of the pro- and anti-hunters.

Radio news bulletins tend to be brief, as they have to fit all their stories into a limited time; 20 seconds are to be allocated to this story.

1 Read aloud the first two paragraphs of the article. Ask a partner to time 20 seconds and then count how many words you have read.

2 Adapt the original article to make your 20-second bulletin.
  a Decide which sections of the original story provide relevant, factual information.
  b Rewrite them until you have a number of words that you can read in 20 seconds.

3 When your story is ready, read it aloud to a partner and ask them to:
- time you – if the timing is wrong, change the wording until it fits
- check that your bulletin is factual – if it contains biased language or opinion you should change them to remove the bias.

Activity 17

A newspaper that is very much against hunting wants to adapt the article and make it into a story that will support the views of the League Against Cruel Sports (LCS). However, there is only space for approximately 100 words.

Write the story. You will need to:
- change the headline
- write a paragraph setting the scene – the what, when and where
- write one or two paragraphs of opinion – about the wrongness of hunting
- include some of the words used by the LCS spokesperson.

Progress check

To show your understanding of bias and objectivity, read the text below about foxes.

1 Write a brief explanation of whether this text is biased or objective in its description of foxes. Comment on:
- the selection and use of facts
- the use or absence of emotive language.

2 Rewrite the following sentences so that they show a bias *against* the fox.
- A survey in Bristol showed that 81 per cent of householders never suffered this nuisance.
- Few householders suffered losses of pets to foxes.
- Cases of foxes killing cats are very rare.

> **Pets and the Urban Fox**
>
> A variety of myths exist about the urban fox. They are reported to cause problems to householders in urban areas, but most householders like to see foxes around and many feed the foxes in their gardens. While foxes are accused of living out of dustbins, a survey in Bristol showed that 81 per cent of householders never suffered this nuisance, and that was before the introduction of wheelie bins. Foxes cannot scavenge from these. The same survey showed that few householders suffered losses of pets to foxes, and that where poultry or small pets, such as rabbits and guinea pigs, are lost, this could be prevented by ensuring safe housing in secure pens and hutches. Foxes generally do not interfere with cats, and cases of foxes killing cats are very rare and mostly unsubstantiated.

Reporting the same event in different ways

The same event will be reported in different ways by different newspapers depending on whom they are writing for.

The two stories on page 28 are reports of the same football match, Stockport County (nicknamed the Hatters) versus Bury (nicknamed the Shakers), which appeared in the newspapers of the two towns involved in the match.

Activity 18

Read the two newspaper stories.

1 What is the main angle on the story of the match taken by the *Stockport Times*?

2 What aspect of the match is the focus for the *Bury Times*?

Teenage striker Adam makes immediate impact

WHIZZ KID   By Mike Bradley

STOCKPORT County assistant boss Mark Lillis was quick to praise Adam Le Fondre after the seventeen-year-old striker came off the bench to fire the Hatters into the second round of the LDV Vans Trophy on Tuesday night.

In an extraordinary game, visitors Bury were reduced to nine men after Chris Porter and Paul Scott saw red – before Stuart Barlow and Le Fondre scored extra-time goals to hand County their first home win since April.

'I was pleased for Adam,' said Lillis, 'He's come on and scored a goal and then hit the bar.

'We've been wrapping him up but he keeps getting injured; he was due to get on the bench, maybe due to start the other week, but he keeps getting these injuries.

'He's only had two days of training but he's an excellent prospect.'

Lillis also confirmed County manager Sammy McIlroy had some harsh words for his side during – and after – the game.

'The gaffer rightly had a little bit of a go at the lads at half time and at the end.

'He thinks a few of them are getting a little bit anxious, but it's a matter of trying to get the lads to be brave and want the ball, and at the moment one or two are not performing well. I think confidence is down but personally I was really pleased for everybody tonight.'

© Stockport Times

'Off' night for Bury!

Shakers' boss Graham Barrow must be wondering whether he's run over a family of black cats, never mind just one, after another cruel defeat on Tuesday night.

The sendings-off of Chris Porter and Paul Scott, not to mention Barrow's banishment to the stands, were the main talking points of a far from ill-tempered first round tie at Edgeley Park.

They took the emphasis off a climactic encounter which saw Jon Daly's opener for Stockport cancelled out by former Huddersfield Town defender Scott, before extra-time goals from substitutes Stuart Barlow and Adam Le Fondre booked County's place in the second round.

'I'm speechless,' said Barrow, who handed a debut to promising young striker Colin Kazam-Richards.

'I'm shocked at what's happened. Chris Porter has been sent off for handball, but he is as honest as the day is long.

'Paul Scott is guilty [for swearing at the official] but I didn't say a word to the referee.

'I'm proud of the players – they were fantastic in the circumstances and they didn't deserve that. It's time it went back to being a man's game.

'When you are sat in the stand and opposing fans come up to you saying, "Unlucky, you didn't deserve that", it speaks volumes. We still had chances to win the game even with ten and nine men.'

But despite defeat Barrow is adamant Bury just need a bit of luck to turn the corner, especially with a series of frustrating results of late.

'It will turn for us, but we've got to believe it's going to turn for us,' he added.

© Bury Times

3 Both newspapers use their headlines to draw attention to their focus.

   a In the *Stockport Times*, which words in the headline draw attention to the youth of the player?

   b Why did they use 'Adam' rather than 'Le Fondre'?

   c In the *Bury Times*, why is 'Off' placed in inverted commas?

   d Why does the headline end with an exclamation mark?

4 Both stories report that two Bury players were sent off. However, they report this fact in different ways. Which of the articles spends most time on this and why?

Sharpen punctuation

Quotation marks in direct speech

Quotation marks are used to show direct speech – words spoken by someone. They are often used in newspaper reports to show that the words in the quotation marks are not the writer's: they are the words of the person who is being quoted by the writer. For example:

When I spoke to the manager he was clearly unhappy with the referee: 'I think that ref was a disgrace!' he told me after the match.

Put quotation marks where they are required in the following passage.

Most of the people I spoke to were very happy with the service they received. The doctors and nurses are lovely, one lady told me.

Using quotations
Activity 19

Many newspaper stories include direct speech – the quoted words of people involved in the story.

1 Which people have been interviewed by the journalist of each newspaper?

2 Why does each newspaper focus on the words of these particular people?

3 In the midst of the quoted words, each story includes some indirect speech:

Lillis also confirmed County manager Sammy McIlroy had some harsh words for his side during – and after – the game.

and

But despite defeat Barrow is adamant Bury just need a bit of luck to turn the corner, especially with a series of frustrating results of late.

Why did two writers include this indirect speech, written by themselves, when they could simply quote what was said?

Photographs and captions
Activity 20
Newspapers often use captions to give meaning to photographs. If you look at the two identical photographs below, you will see that the captions beneath them affect the way you respond to the photograph.

1 'Glory For Britain's Rowers'

2 'Canadian Heroes Give Their All!'

Write a new caption for the photograph from the *Stockport Times* on page 28 that would make the photograph suitable for inclusion in the *Bury Times*.

 Feedback

Here are some details about a Girls' Under-14 schools' football final between Oldchester High School and Newchester Comprehensive:
- at half-time Oldchester were winning 3–0
- after 90 minutes it was a 4–4 draw
- Oldchester won the penalty shoot-out 5–4 to win the match
- Oldchester's captain, Lauren Sutcliffe, scored the winning penalty
- Newchester's Alyson Elliott scored all four Newchester goals but missed her penalty in the penalty shoot-out.

Work with a partner. One of you should write a short report of the match for the Oldchester School Newsletter and the other for the Newchester School Newsletter. You should:
- make up a short, snappy headline
- write a brief report which is written from your own biased point of view to suit the needs of your readers.

When you have written your two reports, compare them.
- Does each report present the facts in a way biased in favour of their team?
- Is the headline short and snappy, and does it attract the interest of the intended audience?

Presentation of stories in different media

Activity 21

Radio news stories are different from those in newspapers because they are listened to rather than read.

1 With a partner, discuss and make notes on the following.
   ● Why are radio news stories usually shorter than those in newspapers?
   ● What advantages do newspapers have in making their stories interesting for readers?
   ● Why might some people prefer to listen to radio news than read a newspaper?

Now read the following national newspaper story.

£1.8bn – the cost of Christmas toys

9 Nov 2004

Parents will splash out around £1.8 billion this year to fulfil their little darlings' wish-lists on Christmas morning, according to research out today.

The figures from Churchill Insurance equate to £150 for each child in the UK.

Children across the country already store more than £7.4 billion worth of toys in their bedrooms, Churchill said.

Excluding items such as clothes and furniture, the contents of the average child's bedroom are worth more than £634 – and Churchill predicts this figure will rise by 23 per cent due to the festive shopping spree.

Churchill's head of home insurance, Martin Scott, said: 'Two-thirds of the nation's parents underestimated the true value of their children's toys in this survey. This can mean millions of pounds worth of uninsured property in the UK.'

The survey stated that four out of five parents say Christmas is all about lavishing the kids with expensive gifts. Books will be this year's number one present for children, closely followed by computer games, board games, money and dolls.

The top ten Christmas gifts are books; computer games; board games; money; dolls; teddies; bikes; footballs; games consoles and mobile phones/DVD players.

Despite parents' free-spending attitude, a staggering 87 per cent of those polled said they felt their children needed to be taught the true meaning of Christmas, as presents seemed to be the most important part of the day.

However, a third admitted they themselves thought that giving and receiving gifts meant more to them than spending time with family and friends or celebrating Christ's birth on Christmas day.

© Manchester Online

2 Explore each of the following statements about the story. Rank them in order, from the statement you can find most evidence for to the one you can find least evidence for. Explain your answers to a partner.
   ● This is a serious story about insurance, reminding readers that they should make sure they have enough insurance.
   ● This is a fun story full of trivial information.
   ● This is a story about how the true spirit of Christmas has been lost and should be found again.

Read the version of the story that was heard on local commercial radio in Coventry.

3 In what ways is the language used here different from the newspaper version. Support your answer with some specific examples.

4 Look back at your answers to question 2. Consider the same three statements in relation to the radio version of the story. Are your answers the same as, or different from, your answers to question 2? Explain why.

> Looks like there's gonna be loads of spoilt kids in Coventry and Warwickshire soon.
>
> Parents are expected to splash out around a hundred and fifty quid per child on pressies this Christmas.
>
> A survey found eight out of ten mums and dads reckon the festive season's all about buying expensive gifts.

Exploring how news stories are influenced by their audience

In the following activities you will explore how radio news bulletins are influenced by the needs of their listeners. News bulletins on the radio are put together from a stream of news that comes into the newsroom. The news team have to:

- select news
- rewrite stories so that they will fit into the available time
- put them in an order that suits the needs of the listeners.

The story below appeared in the news stream coming into the studio of a Coventry local radio station.

> It's emerged the train driver in the Berkshire rail disaster had just two or three seconds to brake before the collision.
>
> An official report says he was rounding a bend at a hundred miles an hour in the dark when he found a car parked on the track.
>
> The 54-year-old driver was among seven people who died in the crash.

This is how the story was re-written:

> The train driver in Berkshire only had two or three seconds to brake.
>
> That's what's come out of the initial investigation into the level-crossing crash that killed 7 people.
>
> The report <u>sez</u> the driver was rounding a bend at a hundred miles an hour in the dark when he found the car parked on the track.

Activity 22

1 Read the two versions of the story aloud while a partner times you. Has the radio version been re-written to make it shorter?

2 Why has the writer of the new version made the changes listed below?
- Dropping 'It's emerged'
- Adding 'the level-crossing crash'
- Dropping the information about the death of the train driver?

3 'sez' is not a proper word. What would this word be in standard English, and why might the script writer working in the radio station have written it in this way here?

Structuring news stories in a bulletin

News on local radio is different from news on national radio. The policy of the local radio station in Coventry is to place news in the following order:

A important and current local news
B important national news
C international news
D less important local stories
E local sports stories
F national sport
G entertainment news

Activity 23

1 Why do you think they order the stories in this way? Do you think local radio is different from national radio?

2 Below and on page 34 is the stream of news that came into a local radio newsroom in Coventry. Work with a partner to decide on the running order according to the criteria above.

> **a** Southampton boss Steve Wigley's under more pressure this morning.
> No win in the Premiership and now a 5–2 thrashing by Championship side Watford in the Carling Cup.
> Arsenal and Spurs join the Hornets in the last 8.
> Portsmouth are in the hat too thanks to a Yak-oo-boo …
>
> **b** We'll hear the initial findings on what caused the Berkshire rail crash later. Seven people died when a high-speed train hit a car on a level crossing near Reading.
>
> **c** 250 people are believed to have died in an air crash yesterday in a remote region of Peru. A British family of three is among those reported missing.
>
> **d** A special meeting of Coventry Council will be held to discuss the Jaguar crisis. 11 hundred and 50 jobs are set to go as Ford ends production at Browns Lane.
> Labour leader John Mutton wants the debate just before before a big march through the city on November 27... 'This could make a huge impact on the city and we've got to challenge it. It's about time for councillors to stand up and be counted; we can't sit back and hope it will all turn out OK. I'll be trying to persuade my fellow councillors to get out and support the march.'

e Looks like there's gonna be loads of spoilt kids in Coventry and Warwickshire soon.
Parents are expected to splash out around a hundred and fifty quid per child on pressies this Christmas.
A survey's found eight out of ten mums and dads reckon the festive season's all about buying expensive gifts.

f A very desperate plea from Amanda Holden.
According to reports she's said she's desperate for her music-producing boyfriend Chris Hughes to make an honest woman of her.
I'm sure that'll get him on his knee … that or make him run away … it's a tough call!

g Text messages are soon gonna be helping to cut the number of sexual health diseases in Coventry and Warwickshire …
The Brook Advice Clinics are now offering help by text.
Penny Barber from there says it'll give a variety of advice … 'We need to be able to help young people cope with a number of different conditions. We hope that by using text messaging we will be able to provide a quick, confidential service using a technology that young people like.'

h Coventry City Reserves drew one all last night at Nuneaton against Charlton.
It looked like it was *gonna* be goal-less till the last five minutes until Craig Pead put the Sky Blues ahead in the 85th minute. But then the visitors equalised a minute later.

When you have decided on the order, compare it with the running order of another pair. Check your order against the criteria given at the start of this activity.

3 Read the news bulletin while your partner times you. Make a note of how long it takes. If the radio station has to cut that amount of time by half, and therefore has to drop some stories, which stories could they cut and still meet the criteria for news selection?

 Progress check

Texts are presented in different ways in different media for a variety of reasons. You have explored the differences between radio news and newspapers and how stories are adapted to suit the needs of particular audiences. The story below is printed in its entirety. When you have read it, decide whether it is most likely to be:

- from a national newspaper
- from a local newspaper
- from a local radio station
- from a national radio station.

Residents of Northumberland Road are going right to the top to fight Council plans to cut down a pair of 200-year-old oak trees. Residents' spokesman Andy Sutcliffe is writing to the Prime Minister in an attempt to save the trees. Environmental Officer Judith Woodfield told us that the trees were in a dangerously fragile state following recent storms and that safety was their main concern.

Write a brief explanation of the features of the story that led you to your answer.

Assessment task

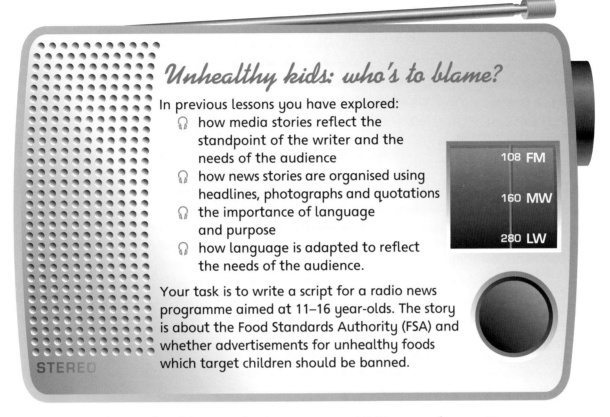

Unhealthy kids: who's to blame?

In previous lessons you have explored:
- how media stories reflect the standpoint of the writer and the needs of the audience
- how news stories are organised using headlines, photographs and quotations
- the importance of language and purpose
- how language is adapted to reflect the needs of the audience.

Your task is to write a script for a radio news programme aimed at 11–16 year-olds. The story is about the Food Standards Authority (FSA) and whether advertisements for unhealthy foods which target children should be banned.

108 FM

160 MW

280 LW

STEREO

The stream of news for this story is given on page 37. You can devote 60 seconds to the story. Your local radio station prides itself on 'balanced' reporting, so the story must reflect equally the views of those who want a ban and those who do not.

The editor wants you to include a snappy headline to introduce the story and to use some non-standard English because the intended audience is quite young.

Step 1
Read the information on page 37. Decide what the main issues are and organise the information into:
- facts about the story
- arguments for a ban
- arguments against a ban.

Step 2
Read some of the sections aloud and time yourself to get an idea of what makes 60 seconds' worth.

Step 3

Choose the material you are going to use. It needs to be written in language that will suit a young audience. Remind yourself of the work you did in Activities 8 and 9. You should consider the following.

- Simplifying some of the wording, for example, 'harness the power of advertising' could be too formal. It could be changed to: 'use adverts to try to change the eating habits of young people'.
- Using quotations but shortening them if they are too long for young people to listen to comfortably.
- Using terms that young people will understand, for example, use 'sweets' rather than 'confectionery'.

Step 4

Decide how you will order your material. You might decide on something like this:

- an introduction to the story
- what those wanting a ban say
- what those against a ban say
- an ending to bring the story to a conclusion.

Step 5

When you have finished your version of the story, check it against the following criteria.

- Have you adapted the language of the source material to suit the needs of young listeners?
- Does your story give a balanced version of the arguments for and against a ban?
- Have you selected quotations that clearly present the views of 'experts' in ways that young people will understand?
- Can your story be read at a comfortable speed in 60 seconds?

 If the answer to any of those questions is 'No', spend a few minutes adapting what you have written. Then read your draft to a partner, who will also check that you have addressed the criteria.

The FSA has suggested that there should be restrictions on food ads which target children. However, it has stopped short of calling for an outright ban.

It says new rules should be introduced to 'address the imbalance' between ads for healthy and unhealthy foods.

There should be limits on ads for 'foods, meals or snacks high in salt, sugar or fat'.

The FSA said the rules should apply during children's TV slots but says extending them 'might also be justified'.

About 40% of ads during children's programmes are for food. Most of these are for confectionery, fast food, pre-sugared breakfast cereals, savoury snacks or soft drinks.

Campaigners say the case for an outright ban is clear.

'It's a cast-iron case as far as we can see,' says Charlie Powell, project officer at Sustain, one of the leading proponents of a ban.

'The food industry spends millions of pounds on these ads because they work. They have been very successful. They influence what children eat.'

However, critics say the scientific evidence is not as clear-cut as some campaigners make out.

'I don't think the scientific evidence presented in the Food Standards Agency report supports its conclusion that ads are influencing children's diet,' says Dr David Ashton, an epidemiologist at Imperial College, London.

'I am not persuaded at all that there is a link. It is convenient to blame large food manufacturers.

'It is much easier than confronting the real issue, which is that decline in physical activity over the last few decades is to blame.'

Those opposed to any outright ban on food advertising are quick to point to the experience of Sweden and the Canadian province of Quebec.

Both have strict laws outlawing food ads which target children.

However, Sweden has similar obesity rates to the UK. Quebec has similar obesity rates to the rest of Canada, where there is no such law.

'The bans have had no impact whatsoever on obesity rates,' says Dr Ashton.

'Some people might want to say that Sweden and Quebec are not typical of the UK. That may indeed be the case.

'But they are the only live experiments on real people that we have and they have not shown any benefit.'

The authors of the FSA report shied away from calling for a ban on junk food ads.

'I wouldn't advocate that at the minute,' says Dr Hastings.

'The danger of banning ads is that manufacturers will simply turn to other channels.'

Dr Hastings believes rather than trying to censor ads, health chiefs should try to harness the power of advertising.

'Marketing has the potential to resolve what is an enormous public health problem,' he says. 'We should be harnessing it as a way of improving diet.'

2 Ways of writing

The bigger picture

In this unit you will experiment with writing poetry of different kinds and explore some of the different ways you can shape stories. At the end of the unit you will plan, draft and revise a short story or poem of your own. You will also read and comment on someone else's piece of work.

WHAT? You will:
- think about how different kinds of poetic structures shape the ideas you wish to express
- explore different ways of structuring stories
- develop your ability to use a range of techniques in your own writing

HOW? by:
- reading and responding to a variety of poems
- writing your own poems using some of the structures of the poems you have read
- reading a range of prose texts to explore how stories are shaped
- writing a variety of narrative prose

WHY? because:
- reading poetry and prose texts by other writers helps you to become familiar with some of the techniques used to shape ideas in interesting ways
- experimenting with different ways of structuring ideas helps to broaden your skills and make you a more effective writer.

Experimenting with form and meaning in poetry

It is quite difficult to give an exact definition of what poetry is, but you can usually spot a poem because of its shape on the page. Poets shape their ideas into lines and stanzas; they use techniques like rhyme to create different effects. In this unit, you will explore simple use of rhyme and experiment with forms such as couplets (two-line poems) and cinquains (five-line poems) to see how they help you to shape ideas.

Rhyming couplets

A pair of rhyming lines can sum up an idea. The second line seems to bring the idea to a close. This is often done for fun:

> **Progress**
> I am a sundial, and I make a botch
> Of what is done far better by a watch.

Hilaire Belloc

Activity 1

Experiment with this form by writing your own couplet. To help you select an idea for your poem, narrow the choice of subject to animals: your poem should make a simple statement about an animal. Two main things will affect the way you shape your idea:

- having to find a rhyme for the last sound of your first line
- the need to have an identical number of syllables in each line ('Progress' has ten syllables in each line).

Choose an animal – a familiar one like a cat or dog, or an unfamiliar one like the extinct dodo. Jot down some key words about your animal: with the dodo the most obvious word might be 'dead' or 'extinct'. Now think of rhymes for these key words, for example:

> *Dead:* said, red, lead, led, bed, head
> *Extinct:* linked, blinked

Start to think how two rhyming words might lead to an idea and shape two lines of similar length. For example:

> Quick as the dodo's eyelids blinked
> These wingless birds became extinct.

or

> With little brain inside its head
> The stupid dodo soon was dead.

When you have written your poem, check that:

- the two lines rhyme
- both lines have the same number of syllables.

How form affects meaning
Activity 2

Poets use more than rhyme to shape their ideas. They break ideas down into lines and shape lines in particular ways on the page. Read the two sentences below.

And so as evening falls I close the curtains on the empty bed. And shadows creep inside.

Now read them again when they are set out in a different way. This time, they are arranged into a five-line poem called a cinquain (from the French *cinq*, meaning 'five').

> And so
> As evening falls
> I close the curtains on
> The empty bed. And shadows creep
> Inside.

Valerie Bloom

1 How do you read these words differently when they are set out as a poem?

2 Do any words stand out more because of the way the poem is set out?

In a cinquain, the poet counts syllables to determine when to start a new line. Cinquains have a strict pattern of syllables: 2, 4, 6, 8, 2. The first four lines get successively longer and are followed by the final short line. Because it is suddenly shorter, it stands out. This means that a cinquain is suitable when you want to explore an idea that can be ended with a short summing-up or a twist.

Write your own
Activity 3

Now write your own cinquain about a time of the day. Follow steps 1–3 below and on page 41.

Step 1

Begin by deciding which time of day you want to focus on. Next, think about the idea you would like to express in your cinquain. For example, you might decide to write about:
- how peaceful the night-time is
- how scary the darkness is
- how hard it is to get up in the morning.

Jot down a simple explanation of the idea you want to explore in your poem.

Step 2

Think of two syllables for the last line. Apart from the obvious words such as *morning, midday, midnight,* you could choose a two-syllable word like *future* or two monosyllabic words like *stone cold*. Now think about how you could lead up to this line.

- You could gradually build up a description and use the last line to sum up the picture you have created – a winter scene leading up to *stone cold*.
- You could use the last line as a surprise or twist – the first four lines could focus on something from the past before a sudden switch to future in the last line.

Step 3

Write your cinquain.

 Feedback

When you have finished your cinquain, show it to a partner together with the explanation you wrote in Step 1. Ask them to assess how successful you have been.

- Is the poem organised into five lines?
- Have you followed the expected pattern of syllables?
- Does the last line stand out – either by summing up the idea you have explored or by giving a twist?

Ask your partner for any suggestions for changing words or expressions in your poem. Rewrite your poem if you are happy with your partner's suggestions. Make sure each line has the correct number of syllables.

Using the contrast between long and short lines to help shape meaning

One way poets vary the length of lines is to contrast long and short lines. Read the poem below.

Why?

We love this beautiful planet.
We love the flowers and bees.
We love the living woods,
The mosses and the trees.
5 We love the buttercups and daisies, oak and elm towering high.
We've just built another motorway.
Why?

Activity 4

1 The first six lines of the poem are a simple list of statements. It is the last line that acts as a 'punch line'. What is the purpose of the last line?

2 Read the longest line again and explain why the writer made that line so long.

3 The words 'We love' are repeated often. What effect does this have on the reader?

4 The fifth line is quite a long list. Why did the writer choose to end it with the word 'high'?

Write your own

Activity 5

You are going to write a seven-line poem with the word 'Why?' at the end. As with the cinquain, the starting point for planning your poem should be the last line. Since the last line is 'Why?', your poem needs to be about something for which you would like an explanation, for example:

- the damage being done to the planet
- rules or manners, showing that the poet doesn't see the point of these rules
- how friends sometimes let us down.

Your poem should include:

- repetition: 'Why?', on page 41, repeated 'We love'
- rhyme: lines 2 and 4, and 5 and 7 of 'why?' rhyme – if it is too difficult to rhyme two pairs of lines you should concentrate on rhyming lines 5 and 7
- at least one very long line, to contrast with the last line.

When you have written your poem, check it against the list of features. If you have not included all of them, redraft the poem.

Sharpen spelling

Using a dictionary and a thesaurus

A dictionary is not the only text you can use to find how to spell words. In a **thesaurus** you will find lists of **synonyms**. Synonyms are words that are very close in meaning. For example, synonyms of *shout* might include *shriek, scream, howl, call*.

1 Use a thesaurus to find synonyms for the words *nice*, *harsh* and *fierce*. When you have found them, copy down **three** words that are unfamiliar to you.

2 Look up your three new words in a dictionary. Design a wall poster that will:
- show the words you began with
- show the synonyms you chose from the thesaurus
- show the dictionary's definition for those words
- offer advice on how to learn the spelling of the words.

You might break down each word into syllables and colour the syllables differently, or you might 'annotate' the word to show how it follows a spelling rule that you are aware of.

Learning how to structure a story in a poem

Just as poetry shapes and influences the development of ideas, it can also be used to shape stories. Whereas in prose, ideas are organised into paragraphs, in poems they can be organised into stanzas. In the activities that follow you will explore further ways of structuring a simple narrative in poetry and prose.

In the poem below the writer uses each stanza to capture a snapshot of a life. Each stanza acts like a paragraph in prose, but the writer shapes lines and uses repetition to create different effects.

That Once Was Me

A tired, weeping toddler
Tiny in the shopping mall.
Calmed by a mother's embrace.
That once was me.

In the corner of Reception
Thumb in mouth, book on lap.
At peace in a fairy-tale world.
That once was me.

A stormy day in March
Daddy's chair empty
Mummy saying we'll be alright.
That once was me.

Standing defiantly outside
The Head's office with bloodied nose.
The injustice of the world.
That once was me.

Frost on the window
Bored in my room.
Missing friends at school.
This now is me.

Activity 6

1 The first two lines in each stanza paint a picture. What is added by each third line?

2 What is the story of the writer's life? Explain the clues in the poem that give you your answer.

3 The first line of the last stanza may be a simple statement of fact, but what extra layers of meaning does it have?

4 What two things might 'stormy' in stanza 3 describe?

Write your own

The form of the poem invites you to paint word pictures from your life. Think of **five** scenes that capture different stages of your life. Make a list of words that could be used to describe each scene. Remember the work you did on using a thesaurus (page 42), and also that words can have more than one meaning: it is important to use words imaginatively.

When you write your poem, especially the first two lines, try to use words and phrases that might suggest layers of meaning to a reader. When you have written your poem, choose one word or phrase that has layers of meaning and explain to a partner what you have attempted to achieve.

The organisation of a story in a pre-1914 poem

The following poem tells a simple story about a fox looking after its cubs. The poet has not divided the poem into different stanzas like 'That Once Was Me', but both poems, like all stories, have a clear beginning, middle and end.

The Vixen

Among the taller wood with ivy hung,
The old fox plays and dances round her young.
She snuffs and barks if any passes by
And swings her tail and turns prepared to fly.
5 The horseman hurries by, she bolts to see,
And turns **agen**, from danger never free.
If any stands she runs among the poles
And barks and snaps and drives them in the holes.
The shepherd sees them and the boy goes by
10 And gets a stick and **progs** the hole to try.
They all get still and lie in safety sure,
And out again when everything's secure,
And start and snap at blackbirds bouncing by
To fight and catch the great white butterfly.

> **Word bank**
>
> **agen** old-fashioned form of 'again'
> **progs** old word meaning 'thrusts' or 'stabs'

John Clare

Activity 7

1 Stories can begin in many ways, but one obvious way is by setting the scene for what is to follow.

   a Summarise in your own words the scene described in the first two lines of 'The Vixen'.

   b Both the first two lines set the scene, but line 1 focuses on a different aspect from line 2. Explain the different focus.

2 What happens in the middle section of this story?

3 Where do you think the middle section of this story ends and, it could be argued, the final stage of the poem begins? Explain your answer.

4 The word 'by' is used four times in the poem. Why is it repeated so often?

5 The word *by* is preceded by the following verbs: 'passes', 'hurries', 'goes' and 'bouncing'. The most vivid of these is *bouncing*. Why do you think the writer chose this word?

6 John Clare uses the simple connective *and* frequently in his poem. Read the following suggestions about why he does this, then decide which one you agree with most. If you feel you have a better suggestion, write that down.

- It is a simple poem about nature: using *and* helps to make the poem seem simple and 'down to earth'.
- Using *and* frequently suggests a build-up of lots of things happening – just as the fox has lots of things to face.
- The word *and* is just a 'filler' to help the writer keep to ten syllables per line.

Progress check

To show your understanding of some of the techniques used in the poems you have explored so far, you are going to rewrite the end of 'The Vixen'. This will test your ability to organise a poem using:

- rhyme (as in the rhyming couplets on page 39)
- syllable count (as in the cinquain on page 40).

Re-read the first ten lines of 'The Vixen'. Think of another way the story could end and then write four lines in the same pattern as the first ten. When you have written your four lines, swap poems with a partner and review each other's work. You should comment on whether your partner's four lines:

- rhyme effectively
- have the correct number of syllables
- provide an effective ending.

Redraft your poem, if necessary, using your partner's suggestions. When you have finished your poem, reflect on the challenge of writing it and answer the following questions.

1 What is difficult about having to shape a story into separate rhyming lines?
2 What are the advantages of organising ideas into separate lines using rhyme?

Exploring beginnings and endings of prose stories

Now that you have examined how a story can be structured in a poem, you are going to look at ways of structuring a story in prose.

Looking at beginnings

Prose writers can begin their stories in many different ways, but openings, however they are written, are very important.

Activity 8

1 A story opening might focus on a particularly important **character**. Make a list of other things a writer might decide to emphasise in the opening to a story. For each of the features on your list, write **one** attention-grabbing sentence for the start of a story. For example, a single sentence focusing on character might begin: 'At six feet four and with a towering temper, Andy Sutcliffe wasn't used to people speaking back.'

2 You are going to read three extracts to explore the different features writers use at the beginning of a story.

Working with a partner, for each text answer the following questions, giving reasons for your answers.

a Does the opening indicate what kind of story it is going to be (romance, adventure, sport, ghost, mystery, etc.)?
For example, *Text C sounds like an adventure – something chasing something. Could be science fiction or fantasy with the strange idea of a city chasing a town.*

b Does the opening give a clear idea of a setting?

c Does the opening introduce what seems to be an important character?
For example, in *Text C no character is mentioned.*

d Does the opening give a clue about a possible plot?
For example, *Text A looks like it is going to be about something that happens in the school holidays and there will be some kind of trouble – 'staying safe'.*

e Does the opening suggest some kind of problem that might need to be resolved?
For example, in Text B: *who killed the dog?*

A

The last minutes of the last lesson of the last day of term were ticking away, and Martin Turner could not wait to be set free. The minutes dragged on as
5 Mr Lincoln, the form tutor, lectured the class on using holiday time constructively, not giving the school a bad name and staying safe.

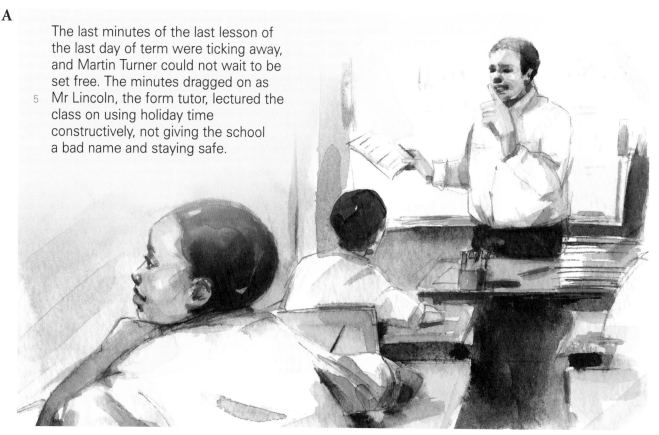

B

It was 7 minutes after midnight. The dog was lying on the grass in the middle of the lawn in front of Mrs Shears' house. Its eyes were closed. It looked as if it was running on its side, the way dogs run when they think they are chasing a cat in a dream. But the dog was not running or asleep. The dog was dead. There was a
5   garden fork sticking out of the dog. The points of the fork must have gone all the way through the dog and into the ground because the fork had not fallen over. I decided that the dog was probably killed with the fork because I could not see any other wounds in the dog and I do not think you would stick a garden fork into a dog after it had died for some other reason, like cancer for example, or a road
10 accident. But I could not be certain about this.

C

It was a dark, blustery afternoon in spring, and the city of London was chasing a small mining town across the dried-out bed of the old North Sea.

3 From your analysis of the three openings, which story might you most want to read? Explain what there is in the opening that might hook you into reading the rest of the story.

Looking at endings

Activity 9

1 The endings to the openings for Texts A, B, and C above are printed below. Match each ending to its opening and explain how you know. Some are obvious because of a character's name, but you should look for further reasons. For example, is there something in the ending that resolves a problem mentioned in the opening?

1

But through the smoke, the steam, the pall of hanging ash he could see nothing, nothing, nothing, and although he swung the binoculars to and fro, growing increasingly desperate, all they showed him were the bony shapes of blackened girders, and the scorched earth littered with torn-off wheels and blazing lakes of
5   fuel and broken tracks lying tangled on themselves like the cast-off skins of enormous snakes.

2

'Well,' Martin replied, 'I feel sorry for my team but I don't feel sorry for myself.' Then Martin stopped. He looked Anthony in the eye and said, 'It's not the winning that
5   matters, or even the taking part. For me, it's the being here. Today I'm the winner.'

3

And I know I can do this because I went to London on my own, and because I solved the mystery of Who Killed Wellington? And I found my mother and I was brave and I
5   wrote a book and that means I can do anything.

2 To show how story openings set up situations that are to be resolved, you are going to work in a group of four looking at openings and beginnings. Each member of the group should write a story opening, remembering to pay attention to the following points.

- What kind of story is it? Adventure? Romance? Science fiction? Ghost story?
- Will you focus on setting? Character?
- How will you hook the reader?

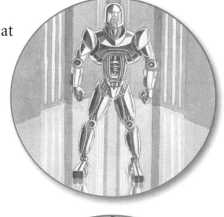

3 Swap your story opening with another member of your group. Read the opening that you receive carefully, looking for clues about:

- what kind of story it is
- what kind of plot has been set in motion
- any important characters who have been introduced.

Now write an ending to the story. When everyone has finished writing, take it in turns to read each opening and its ending. The writers of the endings should explain to the group why they wrote their ending in the way they did. They should explain what there was in the opening that led them to the particular ending.

As each ending is discussed, the writer of the original opening should explain what they had in mind for the rest of the story when they wrote the opening.

Highlight thinking

Creative thinking: elaborating

Elaborating means adding details, explanations or examples. To create a character or a scene, a story writer has to elaborate, choosing and using details that will make the story come alive for the reader.

Elaborating is also important in other sorts of writing, for example:

- a journalist needs to elaborate a news story with details such as eyewitness quotations
- a student needs to elaborate in an essay, using quotations and explanations to develop ideas.

Exploring the ways a writer opens, develops and concludes a short story

You are now going to read a whole short story to investigate how a writer begins, develops and concludes a story. After you have read each section, answer the questions below it.

MOTHER

A bully cannot exist without a victim. His bully-bait. And Robert Spry was pure bully-bait. Small, thin, his glasses held together with sticky-tape after the last time Ashley Polebrook had broken them. It didn't help Robert's cause that he was good at school while his bully most definitely was not. It simply added fuel
5   to the fire – the long slow burn until hometime, when his bully showed him what really mattered in this world was the hardness of the punch or a well aimed kick.

Dim witted, Robert's bully never varied his routine. He always waited in that scrub of spindly trees he knew Robert had to cross, blocking the pathway,
10   pretending at first not to notice Robert, as if Robert was too insignificant.

There he stood now, fists in pockets. Seeing him, even at a distance, brought the tightness to Robert's chest. Yet he knew better than to try to run. He slowed up, then stopped.

'I … I've no money,' he half whispered after a long silence, his eyes lowered
15   and speaking to the ground. He had learned that he couldn't buy off his bully, that the money was taken in an atmosphere of utter contempt which often made his torment worse.

'Who says I *wants* your stinking money?'

1   The writer creates two characters: a victim and a bully. Why does he use the victim's name – Robert – several times but only mention the bully's name once?

2   The start of a story sets up a situation, often a problem that will be resolved later in the story. What is the problem in this story?

3   Write down two possible ways the story might develop. Explain what clues there are in the opening that suggest these developments. You should think about:
    - *what* might happen
    - which *character* the writer would like you to identify with
    - whether the story is going to be serious or light-hearted.

Now read on.

Robert realised he had said the wrong thing. The bully was advancing. Robert
20 felt prickly heat rise from his spine and a second later a blow to his shoulder
sent him stumbling backwards into the mud. His bag fell open and books
dropped out. The bully took pleasure in stamping them further into the mud.
Robert watched him passively, his glasses slightly askew.

The bully snatched up an exercise book fluttering half out of the bag as if
25 trying to fly away in panic.

With a sneer he cast his eyes over Robert's neatly written script on its front
cover and sarcastically read, 'The members of the big cat family by Robert G.
Spry.' Roughly he thumbed its pages, hardly glancing at what was written there,
or at Robert's detailed drawings. Robert winced. Please, he thought, don't
30 damage it. Any of the other books – or even a blow or a kick – but please don't
damage that *one* book.

Several months ago there had been a small class project about big cats,
which for Robert had quickly grown from an interest into a consuming passion.
Even then, of all of the cat family, panthers had been his favourites: they were
35 simply so beautiful. They could kill a man in their stride.

Recognising Robert's passion, Mr Leeson had given him the exercise book
for the specific purpose of recording all his information. Now, most dinner
times, Robert was to be found in the school library searching out even the
tiniest detail about cats; and, of course, the library was one place where his
40 bully never ventured.

Like all expert bullies, Ashley Polebrook sensed the worth to his victim of the
prize he gripped in his hands. Smiling coldly, he held it before Robert's face,
slowly tearing it into four neat pieces and scattering them on the ground. As if
they offended his tormentor's sight, Robert immediately leapt up to clear
45 everything away.

The bully spat into the mud. 'Why don't you just clear off home to your
mummy, Spry?'

Robert paused, looking at him, for a second on the verge of speaking. But
what was there to say? That at home he had tried to explain about his bully to
50 his mother and that all she had said was, 'You must be doing something to
draw attention to yourself'? It was then that Robert realised his mother saw him
as a victim too and thereafter felt only coldness towards her.

4   The victim has been further bullied in a way that you probably
predicted, but the writer has introduced something new: three
paragraphs give details of Robert's interest in big cats and the
importance of the book that the bully destroyed. Guess what
significance this might have later in the story and note down
your ideas.

Read on.

He turned and ran home, if only for the security of solid walls and doors he could lock. In the kitchen his mother was chopping carrots with the same
55   indifference she did everything. She gave him a glance.

'You're all mud,' she said flatly.

'Football.'

'Again?'

'Tripped.'

60   'Plain clumsy.'

She picked up the last piece of carrot and crunched it. Robert watched her, wishing she would ask more, but knowing she wouldn't.

> 5   The writer has introduced a new character: Robert's mother. What impression of her does the reader get?
>
> 6   The writer doesn't tell the reader how to think of the mother; he simply describes things she says and does. Explain what the writer does to shape your impression of the mother.
>
> Read on.

Later, after a silent gloomy meal and an attempt to clean up the mud and repair the ripped book that was way beyond repairing, Robert slipped away to
65   his room. Only here did he feel entirely safe, his mother rarely venturing past its door. As always the room was fastidiously tidy, Robert taking pleasure in order – from the books on the shelf to the shoes by the bed. He kept it so, hoping that his mother might come by and notice …

He switched on his computer, the monitor lighting an otherwise dark room. It
70   was time to transfer today's findings on to disk. Carefully he turned the pieces of mud-stained pages, wondering why the book meant so much to him when most of its details were already logged in his computer and he knew them off by heart in any case. Perhaps it was because he would have nothing to show Mr Leeson – the only one who ever took the slightest interest in him. Tomorrow
75   Robert would have to invent some excuse to explain why he no longer had the book, making sure he didn't implicate his bully in the matter. A good victim never does that.

Angrily Robert found himself striking the keyboard. The screen glowed information. Today at school he had discovered about panther cubs and how
80   they are reared.

He typed: *Panthers can have two maybe three cubs. Panthers make ferociously protective mothers, often defending their cubs to the death …*

He stopped abruptly with a sense of pain, his glasses shining with reflected light.

85   'Panthers will defend *their* own young. They'd fight come what may to protect them. A panther mother wouldn't just stand by and watch *her* cubs being harmed.'

7 What is significant about the details of the behaviour of panthers that Robert sees on the computer screen? How does the information connect with other details in the story?

8 Make another prediction about what is going to happen, then read on.

90 The bitterness of his words spoken aloud to the monitor surprised him. But only for a moment. The computer's screen had suddenly turned into a hissing snow storm of interference. Its brightness made him draw back and its hiss was like that of some living creature. Then, just as abruptly, it failed altogether.

95 Sitting blind before the unresponsive keyboard, Robert felt the darkness brush against him. And more. Something wet and coarse like a tongue was slowly drawing itself across the back of his neck. Frozen with terror, he could hear his blood throbbing and was quite unable to move. Many minutes passed before he was convinced that nothing was there, or ever had been. When finally he dared to move and switched on the light, his room mocked him with its orderliness. For a brief moment Robert felt disappointed.

100 He was awoken the following morning by his mother's scream. As his mother was not one to raise a noise about anything, this added to the urgency of Robert's haste as he dashed downstairs into the kitchen. His mother stood at the half-opened back door. Under her raised arm Robert could see the step and the vividness of blood. Less obvious was the pathetic heap nearby. Robert tilted his head and saw it was a freshly slaughtered lamb.

105 Instinctively he thought of his bully and that it must have been left there by him. But no: Ashley Polebrook was always more direct in his cruelty. Robert took another step forward. The dead lamb, he observed, was set down neatly, almost like an offering. Then, recalling the touch in the darkness like a slow deliberate lick, Robert smiled.

9 The story has taken a strange turn with an unexpected event. Why does Robert smile?

10 The story has almost finished. How do you think the conflict between Robert and the bully will be resolved?

Now read the end of the story.

110 The police hadn't yet arrived about the matter of the dead lamb when Robert set off for school. He didn't mind leaving, for he sensed he carried the drama with him; and as he ran, he felt light headed, revelling in a sense of power. Occasionally he caught a shadowy movement in the bushes alongside the path, keeping in complete step with him.

115   And look. Before him – on the path. Waiting. Ashley Polebrook. His loyal bully.

    Mistaking his speed for an attempt to escape, Ashley grabbed Robert's collar. Robert felt the stitches give.

    'You better let me be, Polebrook,' he said, breathless still from running.

    His unexpected insolence took a while to register in the bully's slow brain
120 and became a contemptuous expression on his face. He yanked Robert closer to him.

    'Why? What you goin' to do about it, Spry? Tell your mummy on me?'

    Robert blinked. 'Yes,' he said softly.

    And in the bushes arose the crackle of twigs and a long deep-throated growl.

by Stephen Elboz

Activity 10

Now that you have read the end of the story, reflect on some of the things you have been considering on your way through it.

1 The bullying incident at the beginning of the story is set by a cluster of trees. Look at the last line of the story again and explain why the writer chose the setting of the bushes rather than any other.

2 Why do you think the writer chose, at an early stage, to make Robert's mother an unsympathetic character? Again, keep the ending of the story in mind when you answer this question.

3 At what stage of the story did the writer introduce the idea of a mother panther being like some kind of fairy godmother, in other words a supernatural character who looks after children?

4 Why do you think the writer called his story 'Mother'?

5 With a partner, discuss the three possible explanations listed below. Decide which one fits the story best.
   a The writer is interested in the subject of bullying and is writing a story to help young people cope.
   b The writer is not really interested in bullying, he is much more interested in the supernatural and wants to thrill readers.
   c The writer wants to entertain readers with a story with a twist.

6 The writer knew the story was going to end with a panther coming to Robert's help. Experiment with other possible closing lines, for example:

Robert blinked. 'Yes,' he said softly.
Out of the bushes sprang a panther which clamped its jaws around the bully's neck.

Write **three** alternative short endings of this type. One of them should be something that in your opinion, does not suit the story. When you have finished, swap your work with a partner and give each other feedback. The feedback should begin either:

This ending could be suitable as an ending because …
or
This ending is unsuitable because …

Exploring point of view

A writer has to decide how to write and shape a story. One major decision concerns point of view. Stories are usually written in the:

- **first person**, using 'I' and 'we' (the action of the story is seen through the eyes of a character *in the story)*
- **third person**, using 'she', 'he' or 'they'. The story is told by a narrator who is outside the story, as though they are looking down on events and can see things from several different points of view.

Each of these has advantages and disadvantages.

Activity 11

1 In a third-person narrative the writer can enter the mind of any of the characters and tell the story from any of their points of view. 'Mother' is a third-person narrative. From how many points of view does the writer tell this story?

2 Below are two examples of a writer experimenting with ways of telling a story. The writer is trying to decide whether to use the first or third person. Read the two examples and write down the advantages and disadvantages of each.

- *I was waiting by the school gates. John appeared and told me about the fight in the canteen. Apparently …*
- *Emily was waiting by the school gates. In the canteen John walked up to …*

3 When you write a story in an English lesson, what makes you choose to use the first or third person?

Sometimes a story is told from two different points of view. *Ruby Tanya* is a novel by Robert Swindells. The plot concerns asylum seekers. The writer chose to tell the story from alternating points of view with two first-person narrators. Both are girls, one of whom is an asylum seeker.

Read the two opening chapters of the novel.

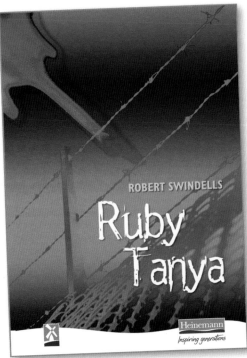

ROBERT SWINDELLS

Ruby Tanya

Heinemann
Inspiring generations

One: Ruby Tanya

The bomb went off when we were all outside waiting for the prince, so that was lucky. He wasn't coming to see us: he had to drive through Tipton Lacey to get to the camp and the road goes right past the school, that's all. He was due at the camp at half-past two, so he'd pass us a few minutes before. At quarter
5   past, the teachers gave us a little flag each and lined us up along the fence, which is only three metres from the road. I felt such a plonker I wished it was three miles.

My dad loves the royals. He says they're part of what makes England the best country in the world. Mum quite likes them too, even though *her* mum's a
10 hippy who says royalty's a rip-off. We went to Buckingham Palace loads of times when I was younger. Outside it, I mean. We never actually went *in*. We went to Sandringham too, and Windsor, and Balmoral. Dad once thumped someone in a pub for calling the Queen a parasite. Two policemen came to the house. Mum thought they'd come to take him to prison, but they just talked to
15 him for a few minutes. I had to go up to my room so I don't know what they said, but I was a bit disappointed when I saw them leave without him.

He's not chuffed about today's visit though, because he doesn't like asylum seekers. At breakfast he says, What's he visiting that scruffy camp for? He'd be better off looking round the village, popping into school, seeing how packed it
20 is now *their* brats've taken over. Dad reckons the school will start going downhill because of the asylum seekers' kids. Mum says everything'd be cool if we let real asylum seekers stay and sent economic migrants back. I try not to get involved in their fratching, it does my head in.

There weren't any asylum seekers' kids in school that afternoon, which is a
25 shame because that's what started the trouble. They'd all got a half-day off to meet the prince at the camp.

Anyway there we were, the rest of us, lined up waiting with our little Union Jacks, and suddenly there's this terrific bang. Not *just* a bang: there was something else, something invisible that slammed me into the fence and hurt
30 my ears and took all the air away. I didn't think, *What the heck was that?* I thought, *Maybe this is how you feel when a prince goes by*. How sad is that?

For a few seconds there was just the noise of things falling on the ground, like rain. Then the screaming started, and the shouting. I was lying on the grass with my cheek pressed up against the fence. I wasn't injured, just sort of
35 dazed; couldn't get myself together to move my head so the fence'd stop hurting my cheek. I heard somebody – a teacher, I suppose – call out, My God look at the *school*. I didn't look. I could see across three metres of grass to the road and I saw the prince pass by. Or at least I saw his car. Long and black it was, with gleaming wheels. It didn't slow down; in fact it seemed to speed up,
40 and I bet I was the only one who spotted it.

One or two of the kids were quite badly hurt and Mr Conway the student teacher had vanished completely, but I didn't know that then.

Two: Asra

We were very happy because the prince will visit our camp. When even a prince has seen us, spoke with us, how can they send us away? That is what my
45 mother and all of the older people were saying. Everybody was working very hard to make the camp look nice so the prince will see we are clean people, and proud. We children have practise a song of our country to sing for him as well, though none of us wants to go back there because of the bad men.

It does not happen, this visit we all want so much, because of the explosion.
50 The prince was coming, his motor car was very close when the explosion did damages at my school. The policemen think maybe somebody bad is trying to blow up the prince, so they turn his motor car round and hurry him away. A man comes to tell us the visit is cancelled, and also that the school will be closed tomorrow because of this explosion. He says children are hurt, a man is
55 missing. It could be a gas explosion, or a bomb.

At six o'clock everybody is at the social club to see the TV news. The very first bit is about Tipton Lacey and it isn't gas, it was a bomb. The prince was only four hundred metres away when it went off. Two pupils have suffer perforated eardrums, a student teacher is missing. An investigation is under
60 way. The police are having an open mind, but the possibility that this was a terrorist attack by a Muslim fundamentalist group cannot be ruled out.

We are all shocked, and also very sad. What sort of person blows up a school? What if the bomb had gone off ten minutes earlier or ten minutes later, with all the children inside?

65 Not *all* the children, says Mr Shofiq, our leader here at the camp. He looks worried. Not all the children were inside ten minutes earlier, and they wouldn't have been inside ten minutes later either, and that's dangerous.

Why? somebody asks. What d'you mean?

Mr Shofiq shakes his head. *Our* children, he says. None of our children was at
70 school this afternoon. The Muslim children. No Muslim child could possibly have been in the school when the bomb exploded, or anywhere near it. They were here, every one of them. Safe and sound. I'm afraid some people are going to call that a strange coincidence.

You mean …?

75 Yes, of course, said Mr Shofiq. We are not so popular in Tipton Lacey, are we? You mark my words: sooner or later somebody is going to suggest that perhaps we planted the bomb.

But why *would* we? cried the other man. We want to stay in England, make our homes here. Also it is our children's school, where they are learning
80 English; learning to *be* English. We'd have to be insane even to *dream* of …

Mr Shofiq nodded. You're right, we'd have to be insane, but you see, a lot of people think that's exactly what we are: mad bombers with beards and turbans. When people die, when children are hurt, people don't think. They don't take the *time* to think. The tabloids wind them up, point them in a certain direction
85 and they go on the rampage. He shook his head. Believe me, there are dangerous times ahead. We must prepare ourselves.

I was so, so scared when Mr Shofiq said these words. I hoped he was mistaken, *prayed* that he was, but he wasn't. I suppose that's why we made him our leader.

Making the two first-person 'voices' different
Activity 12

When a story is told by two first-person narrators, the writer needs to make them easily distinguishable.

1 Ruby's first language is English, whereas Asra is learning English.
Here are some differences you might expect to find in their language use.
- The non-native speaker might make mistakes and be less fluent.
- The native speaker might use more slang or colloquial language.
- When reporting what other people say, the native speaker might find it easier to put what has been said into her own words. The non-native speaker might find that difficult and might simply repeat the words without changing them.

Using these three points to help you, explain how the writer has made the two 'voices' different. Give examples to support what you write.

2 By creating two different points of view, the writer also creates two very different characters. Compare Ruby and Asra by discussing the following with a partner:
- their attitudes towards adults
- their feelings about the prince's intended visit
- their responses to the bomb.

Write down evidence from the text to demonstrate Asra's and Ruby's different attitudes.

When two first-person narrators are describing the same event, the reader could become bored because they are reading the same thing twice. So the writer must make their two narrators' versions different.

When a writer uses two first-person narratives the reader can begin to see future conflicts in the story because of the differences in their points of view. For example, the two accounts suggest different feelings about asylum seekers.

 Sharpen spelling

Learning prefixes
One good way to learn spellings is to become aware of prefixes that are the same in lots of words. For example, the word 'parasite' appears in *Ruby Tanya* (line 13).

1 Many words begin with the prefix *para-*. List **ten** words that begin in this way.
2 Look in the dictionary to see if there are any words that begin *parra-*.

This same tip can help you to learn even harder words. For example, if you learn the prefix 'psych-', it will help you learn a lot of other words.

3 How many other words can you spell that begin with this prefix?

3 a From Ruby Tanya's version of the explosion, read the two paragraphs beginning, 'My dad loves the royals' (lines 8–23).

- What ideas about asylum seekers are explored in this section?
- What are Ruby's views of these ideas?

b What different view of asylum seekers does the reader get from reading about things from an asylum seeker's point of view?

c From your reading of the two sections that begin the novel, what kinds of things do you think will happen as the story develops?

d It would be possible to write any story with more than one narrator. Why do you think the writer chose to tell this particular story from two points of view?

> ### Highlight thinking
>
> **Creative thinking: awareness of different perspectives**
> Trying to understand other people's thoughts, feelings and ideas is a very important skill. In your English work this will help you to:
> - improve listening and communicate effectively in discussion
> - develop imaginative and vivid detail in your writing
> - understand and respond to other people's writing.

4 Attempt your own short version of a story with two different narrators. For example, you could imagine a playground fight or argument. Your two narrators are:

- a teacher who sees it
- one of the students involved in the fight/argument.

Alternatively, think of your own scenario.

You are only going to write one or two paragraphs, not an entire story. Before you start to write, think about:

- how you can make your narrators different by giving them different kinds of language and ways of thinking
- how you can make the two versions of the same event interesting to the reader
- how you can introduce a problem between the two different points of view.

Progress check

Mark your own story against the following criteria:
- making the language of the two 'voices' different
- making the characters different in their thinking/actions
- making the writing interesting by giving different versions of the same event.

Mark your writing by underlining or highlighting words/phrases that show you successfully meeting the three criteria above. In the margin, write 'language', 'character' or 'event' to indicate which criterion your highlighted section relates to.

At the end of your piece of writing, award yourself a mark out of 5 where 1 = uncertainty about all of the criteria and 5 = great confidence about all three. Explain your mark.

Assessment task

Read the following advertisement requesting short story and poetry submissions for an anthology aimed at teenage readers.

EXPRESS YOURSELF: Issues!

We are putting together an anthology of writing by young people about what their lives are like at the start of the 21st century. You can either submit a poem or a short story. Your story can have more than one narrator.

Your writing will be selected for publication based on the following:
- a strong opening that establishes character, setting and/or a problem to be resolved
- a short, punchy ending
- effective use of language
- exploration of issues and ideas relevant to life at the start of the 21st century.

Read the following guidelines before you start.

1 Think about a story that focuses on a real-life situation and features a young person. Ideas may come from your own life, from things you have heard about from friends, or from things in the news. You could consider stories about bullying or peer pressure, the problems that arise between young people and adults, or youth crime.

2 Decide whether you wish to write something based on a true story or made up.

3 Decide what approach you wish to try: poetry, or a short story.

Poetry

If you decide to write poetry you are asked to write a poem:
- organised into separate stanzas
- in which lines have similar numbers of syllables (although, of course, for good reasons you may deliberately vary the number of syllables in certain lines)
- in which there is some use of rhyme
- that has an opening to 'hook' the reader and a satisfying ending.

Prose

If you decide to write a short story in prose:
- you should begin by thinking of your ending
- your opening should set the scene, introduce the main character(s) and give the reader a clue about the problem the story will explore
- you should decide whether you will tell the story in the first or third person, or whether you will use two voices. You should think about why you have chosen your approach.

Step 1

The first stage of your planning for this task should be to note down some ideas in response to the points on the previous page. In particular you should make sure you have noted how your short story or poem will end.

Step 2

Write a first draft quite quickly. This should be not more than 500 words long for the short story and a minimum of ten lines if you are writing a poem.

Step 3

Now do the following.

- Carefully re-read your opening paragraph or stanza. Different kinds of story have different kinds of openings. Does your opening do any of the following?
  - Set the scene.
  - Create a conflict to be resolved.
  - Introduce an interesting character.
  - Use language effectively to have an effect on the reader.

- Read your ending. Does it provide a satisfying ending to the story?
- Proofread your writing to check the accuracy of your:
  - spelling
  - paragraphing or stanza division.

Step 4

You are now ready to write your final draft.

Reviewing

It is important to the publisher that they test out the effectiveness of the pieces of writing in their anthology. You must now read one of the entries written by someone you know and write a brief response by copying and completing this feedback form.

Title and writer: ....

Outline the story and the form in which it is told. Comment on the effectiveness of the opening and the ending:

- Does the beginning of the story give clues about what kind of a story it is going to be? ....

- Does the opening create an interesting character, setting or situation? ....

- Are there any clues that guide the reader to the ending? ....

- How does the story end, and is it a satisfying ending? ....

Give details of any suggestions you might have that would improve it. ....

3 Active communication

The bigger picture

In this unit you will develop effective listening and interviewing skills and practise communicating your ideas effectively in writing and speaking. You will explore different ways of making notes and commenting on them in an extended piece of writing. At the end of the unit you will use the skills you have developed to make notes on a range of texts before discussing and presenting your ideas as a group.

WHAT? You will:
- develop your skills as a listener and speaker
- review your note-making skills
- read unfamiliar texts and make notes on them
- shape material to meet the needs of your readers

HOW? by:
- identifying key points in texts you have listened to
- combining information from your notes into a new text
- putting forward your point of view clearly and coherently in a group discussion
- planning your work carefully to match the needs of your audience and your purpose

WHY? because:
- you need to be a confident speaker and a sensitive listener in many situations, both in and out of school
- note-making is a skill that is especially useful in helping you to prepare for tests and exams
- using information gained from reading to produce your own writing will help you with a wide range of school subjects.

Developing listening skills

It is important to listen to others, but sometimes it can be hard to concentrate and remember what they said. The following activity will help you to develop your skills as a listener. Working with a partner, you will take it in turns to read sections of a text. At the end, if you have listened carefully, you should be able to identify key points.

Activity 1

1 Work in pairs. One of you is **A** and the other is **B**. **A** will read Text A below and **B** will close the book and listen, but can make notes if he or she wishes. **A** should read the information aloud, clearly and slowly. At the end of the reading **B** will be asked to identify:

  a the number of endangered species
  b the causes of decline in the species
  c at least two species on the Critically Endangered list.

Text A

Red Alert

More than 15,000 animals and plants are in danger of extinction according to a new report.

This month the RED List from the IUCN – the World Conservation Union – revealed that 15,589 species are either critically endangered, endangered or vulnerable – that's an increase of 3,300 species.

'The situation facing these species is serious and getting worse. We must refocus and rethink the way in which society must respond to this global threat,' said Achim Steiner, the IUCN director-general.

Causes of the decline in these species include deforestation, habitat destruction and climate change.

Of the 7,266 animals and 8,323 plants named:
  ○ 42 per cent of turtle and tortoise species
  ○ 32 per cent of amphibian species
  ○ 23 per cent of mammal species
  ○ 12 per cent of bird species
are under threat.

Among the species on the Critically Endangered list are:
  ○ Chinese alligator
  ○ Bonin fruit bat
  ○ Philippine eagle
  ○ Brazilian guitarfish
  ○ Kouprey.

2 Now swap roles. This time **B** is the reader and **A** is the listener. **B** should read the following information aloud, clearly and slowly. At the end of the reading **A** should provide:

    a three reasons why the gorillas are an endangered species

    b the number of gorillas in the mountain gorilla population

    c the cause of a decline in population for the western lowland gorilla.

Text B

Gorillas

The largest of the great apes, the gorilla, is among our most endangered species. Having endured decades of civil war in Central and East Africa, gorillas are now faced by the devastating consequences of habitat loss. There is also danger from poaching for the bushmeat trade and the spread of dangerous diseases like Ebola.

The fate of different species varies. The mountain gorilla population, which had been on the edge of extinction, now totals more than 700 individuals and is beginning a slow increase. But the western lowland gorilla faces a severe Ebola crisis, which recent reports show has caused a 56 per cent decline in population across its range. Some of the hardest hit areas have suffered even more than this.

3 With your partner, discuss what you found difficult about the activity. Did you use any techniques to help you remember what you had heard?

Developing your interview techniques

Asking the correct questions

To be a good listener you have to be good at asking questions. Asking questions is a good way of getting clear information.

An interview is a series of questions designed to get particular answers. You may already use interview techniques in some of your lessons such as role play in drama or conducting a survey in design and technology. Interviews can be used for many different purposes.

With a partner, list as many different types of interviews as you can and talk about the purposes of each one. The following three illustrations give you some clues.

The art of being a good interviewer depends on asking questions that will give the kind of answers you want. The policewoman wants to know who committed the crime. The chat-show host wants to find out about the celebrity's life. The questions they ask will build on what they have already heard.

Think about the differences between these two questions:

Were you at Blagdon Station at nine o'clock last night?

What were you doing between eight and ten o'clock last night?

The first of these questions requires only a 'yes' or 'no' answer. The policewoman finds out very little about the suspect's movements. This is a **closed** question.

The second question makes the suspect describe their movements over a period of time, giving a lot more information. This is an **open** question.

Activity 2

Two Year 9 students were asked to perform a role play; one of them was a chat-show host and the other was a celebrity. The interview did not go very well, because the questions asked were all closed questions. Their questions are shown in the table below. Copy and complete the table, changing each one into an open question. The first one has been done for you.

Closed question	Open question
Did you have a happy childhood?	Could you tell me about one of your happiest childhood memories?
Do you have a favourite film?	
Were you a good student at school?	
Do you like music?	

Feedback

1 Work with a partner and ask them the closed questions first. Record their answers.
2 Now ask the open questions. These should produce more interesting answers. If they don't, you need to change them in a way that will produce a more detailed response.

Planning and carrying out an interview

You have practised asking questions that help your partner give detailed answers. Your next task is to plan and carry out a longer interview. In order to do this you need to develop your skills in prompting your interviewee and following up on their answers. This requires good listening skills.

Prompting

Sometimes interviewees can be shy at answering questions. They may hesitate, especially for the first few questions. As an interviewer it is your job to put them at their ease and prompt them if they are unsure of what to say next. Look at the example below.

Interviewer: Do you have any memories of good times at school?
Interviewee: Oh yes, there are so many I'm not sure which one to tell you about.
Interviewer: Perhaps you went away on a school trip …
Interviewee: The ski trips were the best, especially the time we went to Quebec.

Follow-up questions

Sometimes an interviewee's answers can be rather short. If you ask a follow-up question you can extend their answers and make the interview more interesting. Look at these examples of follow-up questions. They could have been used to continue the interview above. Which one do you think would be best to use?

a Interviewer: What do you most enjoy about skiing?
b Interviewer: I've never been to Quebec. What's it like?
c Interviewer: What was it about the ski trips that you most enjoyed?

Activity 3

You have been asked to take part in a TV programme called *Your Future, My Future*, in which young people talk about their ideal life in ten years' time. Work with a partner to design the questions and carry out an interview.

Follow steps 1–3 on page 69.

Step 1

With a partner, work out the questions you will ask the interviewee. You could ask about
- work
- partners
- travel
- holidays
- interests
- home
- possessions.

Remember to ask open questions that focus on the person's ideal life in ten years' time.

Step 2

Structure your interview. Decide :
- how you should open your interview
- the order of your questions
- how you should close your interview.

Step 3

Carry out your interview. Decide who will be the interviewer and who will be the interviewee. If you are the interviewer, make sure you:
- help your interviewee to give extended answers by prompting them
- follow up interesting answers with follow-on questions.

If you are the interviewee, make sure you:
- listen carefully to each question
- develop your answer to make it interesting.

 Feedback

Together, assess how well the interview went by answering the following questions.
1 Did the questions that you wrote enable the interviewee to say all they could say about their ideal life in ten years' time? Give reasons for your answers.
2 How did the interviewer's prompts and follow-on questions help the interviewee?
3 Was there a clear opening and closing to the interview?
Decide how your questions and questioning technique could be improved.
Change places so that the interviewer becomes the interviewee and re-do the interview.

Exploring ideas in a group

Group discussions take place for a variety of purposes, for example a debate in Parliament about new laws, or a discussion among students when planning group work. With a partner, talk about other situations where group discussions take place and the purpose of them.

Group discussions can be difficult. Sometimes everyone can talk at once and it's hard to hear. Sometimes quieter people don't get a chance to speak when they want to. To make sure that a group works well in discussions it is a good idea to draw up some rules first.

Activity 4

1 On your own, write down **four** rules that you think are necessary for small group discussion.

2 Share your ideas with three or four more students. Have you thought about:
- whether you should have someone in charge (chairperson)
- how quiet people can be drawn into the discussion
- what to do about people who keep interrupting
- how to cope with people who don't contribute
- how to keep a record of the group's discussion?

Together, decide the **five** most important rules for your group to work well together.

Activity 5

1 On your own, read and think about whether you agree with the list of statements about happiness on page 71.

2 Share your ideas with your group. *Everyone* must have a chance to speak. If you do not agree with other members of your group you may have to go with the **majority**. This means accepting the decision made by the greatest number.

3 Sort the statements into three groups:
- statements we agree with
- statements we disagree with
- statements we are not sure about.

What is happiness?

a It's what we're all searching for.

b It's what we already have.

c It's something that's always round the corner: when you're nine it's turning ten, when you're fourteen it's turning sixteen.

d It's enjoying what you have now.

e It's getting what you want.

f It's a process of accumulating more and more pleasures or fun experiences.

g It's something you are when you finally get enough cool clothes.

h It's something that is temporary, brief, momentary.

i It's something you'll have when all your dreams come true.

j You can never be completely happy.

k It's something that's different for everybody.

l It's something you learn more about as you go through life.

m You can't choose happiness, it just comes to you.

n You have to catch happiness yourself.

4 In your groups select **four** statements you agree with. For each one, record two reasons why you agree with it. Select a spokesperson who will explain these to other students.

✓ Progress check

In this progress check you will assess what you learned about speaking and listening. You will focus on how well you have worked in your group.

1 Ask yourself the following questions.
- Did I listen to other people?
- Did I say which statements I agreed and disagreed with?
- Did I give reasons for my choices?
- Did I ask appropriate questions?
- Did I help the spokesperson to make notes?

2 Award yourself a mark from 1 to 5, where 5 = excellent, for each of the above questions.

3 Choose the two areas where you got the lowest marks. Write a short report explaining why you did not do well and what you could do to improve.

4 Write a list of advice (four to five points) for classroom display, telling other students how to carry out a successful group discussion.

Making notes

Note-making is a skill you need in lots of subjects in school. It helps you to:
- identify key points in a text
- prepare for tests and exams
- prepare and plan for a piece of writing or a presentation.

Activity 6

1 Look at the example below and list the note-making techniques used.

 Henry VIII's wives

Name	Rel.	Married	Got rid of?	Notes
Catherine A.	RC	1509	Div.	Was married to Hen's <u>bro</u>.
Anne B.	P	1533		Had an <u>affair</u>, poss. a witch
Jane Sey.	RC	1536	R.I.P	Had Hen's only <u>son</u>

Some note-making formats are better suited for some tasks than others. You need to know a range of formats so you can select the one that you find most helpful for the task.

2 With a partner, list as many different note-making formats as you can. There is one example below to help you. When making notes the most important things are that:
- your notes are short and to the point
- you can understand your notes and use them later.

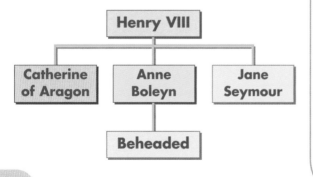

Sharpen spelling

Adding suffixes

The suffix *-ous* means 'full of'.
- when *-ous* is added to a word that ends in a consonant, there is no alteration to the original word, e.g. *joy* → *joyous*
- words ending in silent *e* drop the *e* before adding *-ous*, e.g. *nerve* → *nervous*
- if a word ending in *e* has the soft sound *g* at the end, e.g. *courage*, the *e* is retained before *-ous*, e.g. *courageous*
- words that contain the vowel *u* drop the *u* when an *-ous* ending is added, e.g. *humour* → *humorous*
- when *-ous* is added to a word with a soft *c* sound, for example *spa<u>c</u>e*, the final *e* is replaced by an *i*, e.g. *spacious*
- when *-ous* is added to a word ending in *-y*, e.g. *fury*, the *y* is replaced by an *i*, e.g. *furious*.

Add *-ous* to the words below, making any necessary changes to the root word.

**glamour   prosper   grace   glory   virtue
outrage   advantage   adventure   mountain**

Activity 7

1 Read and make notes on the text below, which is about bullying. Remember to use the note-making format that you find most useful for this task.

Bullying can include both verbal and physical abuse. It can also include theft, threatening behaviour and **coercion**. Bullying has a very negative effect on pupils' sense of well-being and personal safety at school and can result in serious loss of **self-esteem** and confidence for the victims. Bullying can make a child's life at school an extremely miserable experience and can at times be very frightening indeed.

Victims who suffer bullying are often singled out for their physical characteristics such as their size or their appearance. They are often perceived as children who are vulnerable in some way and who may not be able to stand up for themselves.

Children who bully do so for a variety of reasons. Sometimes they have a low sense of **self-esteem** which they can boost by bullying. They may be pupils who find it difficult to make friends and to relate to others. It is also possible that they come from families where physical aggression is encouraged. In some cases children who have been victims of bullying in the past have become bullies themselves.

Research reveals that bullying is widespread. In a recent ChildLine survey just over half of both primary (51%) and secondary school pupils (54%) thought that bullying was 'a big problem' or 'quite a big problem' in their schools. Name-calling was reported as the most common form of bullying for pupils in both Years 5 and 8. Bullying involving physical aggression was less common but was reported by a substantial proportion of pupils in both age groups. Boys and girls seemed to share experiences of bullying. Similar numbers of boys and girls reported physical bullying, name-calling and being excluded by their friends. Some forms of physical bullying were higher for boys in Year 8.

The ways in which schools respond to bullying can vary. According to pupils in the survey, the most effective schools were those which had teachers who were willing to listen and to act appropriately on the suggestions of pupils. Whilst some schools adopted one-off **initiatives** such as discussing the topic in assemblies or lesson times, the ones that were felt to be most effective were the ones that had developed on-going approaches such as appointing anti-bullying counsellors or had teachers with special anti-bullying responsibilities.

The most effective responses to bullying as identified by the pupils themselves were: learning to be assertive with the bully and standing up for yourself, using your friends to help you, telling teachers or parents and using avoidance strategies.

Word bank

coercion force
self-esteem a good opinion of oneself
initiatives introductory acts or steps

2 Compare your notes with a partner's.
Check that you have:
- included the same key points
- used abbreviations
- not written in sentences
- not written in too much detail.

3 Add to or change your notes to improve them.
This could include making your notes shorter.

Making notes on a range of texts

Sometimes you need to take information from a range of texts. To do this you need to make notes on each of them. You will consider different ways of doing this in Activities 8 and 9.

Activity 8

You are going to read four texts on the subject of happiness and make notes on them. You will then use your notes to help you write an article for a parents' magazine. Your article will be about children's happiness.

1 Look at the list of note-making methods below. Which one would best help you to gather information on the subject? List them in order of preference.
   - **a** Read all the texts through twice and then make the notes mainly from memory, only checking if something has been forgotten.
   - **b** Read the texts once, then read them again, looking for key words before making the notes.
   - **c** Decide on a group of headings that suits the subject. Read each text and make notes under each heading before moving on to the next text.
   - **d** Decide on a group of headings that suits the subject. Use all the texts to make notes under one heading. Move on to the next heading.

2 Compare your list with a partner's and explain why you chose the order you did.

Sharpen spelling

Acronyms and abbreviations
Text B, 'What young people think'(page 76), comes from a report by Unicef (the **U**nited **N**ations **I**nternational **C**hildren's **E**mergency **F**und). Words like this, formed from the initial letters or parts of words making up a pronounceable name, are known as **acronyms**.

1 Write out the full version of these acronyms. (You may need a dictionary to help you.)
   **ABTA   AIDS   AWOL   UEFA
   RADAR   LASER   RAM**
You will also be familiar with **abbreviations** where a group of letters is used to represent the whole word. For example, PE stands for Physical Education.

2 What are the meanings of the following abbreviations?
   **GCSE   BBC   IQ   ER   PA
   DVD   GB   CV   BMX**

Activity 9

Closely read Texts A–D on pages 75–6. They are reports on research about children's happiness. Make notes under the following sub-headings:

- reasons for happiness
- causes of unhappiness
- age differences
- differences between boys' and girls' attitudes to happiness
- conclusions from the reports.

Remember to:

- keep your notes brief
- select key points
- abbreviate words.
- record which text your notes are taken from

To help you structure your note-making and focus your thoughts, ask yourself the following questions.

- What information do I want to give my readers about the reports?
- What order will I present my ideas in?
- How will I link my ideas?
- What comments will I make about the reports?

Text A

Hold the pocket money

What makes children happy? If you thought more pocket money would do it, think again. A recent study shows that wealth plays no part in making young people feel good.

The report from York University asked 1,300 children, aged eleven to fifteen, how often they felt unhappy or depressed. Their answers revealed that poor children are just as happy as teenagers from wealthy homes. And pocket money made no difference to their happiness. Professor Jonathan Bradshaw, one of the authors of the report, said: 'Pocket money makes no difference to happiness. Children's income did not appear to matter and neither did their parents' income.'

If children said they were unhappy or depressed on at least four days a month, the survey categorised them as 'sad'. Some things were more likely to make children feel this way. For example, teenagers get more miserable as they get older. They are four times as likely to be sad at the age of fifteen than eleven. The sex of the child is also important – girls are often more unhappy than boys. And pressure to fit in with their classmates can make girls feel blue.

Text B

What young people think: Europe and Central Asia

Two-thirds of all children polled feel happy most of the time. In general, girls feel happy more often than boys, and children who live in towns are happier than those who live in the countryside.

Being with friends is a major source of happiness (61 per cent particularly in Western Europe). This is followed by being with family (54 per cent), doing well in school (especially for girls and younger respondents) and playing or having free time (especially for younger children and boys).

On the other hand, leading sources of unhappiness include being punished or scolded (5 in 10), getting poor marks in school (over 4 in 10), and problems or quarrels at home (3 in 10). Children worry most about family problems (45 per cent) and doing badly in school (42 per cent). Other worries include the environment, politics, war and future employment.

Text C

The Success Report 2004 – key findings

Success is happiness – The vast majority of young people (93 per cent) believe 'doing something you enjoy is more important than making a lot of money'. Only 6 per cent see lots of money in the bank as a sign of success.

Text D

Happiness in the news

A new study of young people's well-being released today by NEF (the New Economics Foundation) shows that young people's well-being drops drastically at secondary school, with significant effects on their personal development.

Sixty-five per cent of primary school children rate their school experience as positive, whereas this drops by more than half to 27 per cent at secondary school. Satisfaction at school is an important part of a child's development.

Young people who said sport was their favourite activity had significantly higher well-being than those who didn't.

Well-being falls a lot as children get older. While 9 per cent of children have low satisfaction and low personal development, this rises to 16 per cent at age twelve to fifteen. Girls suffer a significantly greater drop in the personal development measure than boys.

Commenting on a text

When you turn your notes into writing, you may need to add your own comments to explain and interpret the information for your reader. You need to expand on your initial statement to help your reader develop a clearer understanding. For example, the statement: **'Wealth plays no part in making young people feel good'**, could be followed by the comment: *This suggests that young people feel that money is not all that important.*

This is the opinion of the writer and goes beyond the research findings. Notice that it is introduced by the phrase 'This suggests …'. Other useful phrases for introducing your own comments are:

- 'This seems to show …'
- 'This implies …'
- 'This may indicate …'

Activity 10

1 This activity will help you comment on the information in the reports.

Read the following statements.

- 'Well-being falls a lot as children get older.'
- 'Children worry most about family problems.'

For each one, write a comment in which you try to explain and interpret the statement for your reader. Use the phrases above to help you introduce your comments.

〝 Sharpen punctuation

Using a comma

You will already know that the comma has a range of uses. One use is to separate the opening phrase from the rest of the sentence. Look at this example from Text B:

'In general, girls feel happy more often than boys.'

1 Copy out the sentences below, putting in a comma.

- In the first place it has to be stated that the majority of children like school.
- In my opinion girls enjoy sport just as much as boys.
- On the other hand homework could be said to be harmful to students because it robs them of their free time.

2 Another way of introducing comments is to make your personal opinion very clear by using the personal pronoun 'I' and the possessive pronoun 'my'. Look at the statement below and the comment written about it.

'Playing or having free time is especially important for younger children and boys.'

From my own experience I think this is true. As I got older I realised I had to spend more time on my homework than playing.

The personal and possessive pronouns have been highlighted. Notice how the writer draws on personal experience to support the comment.

Write a comment in response to each of the three statements below:

- using at least one personal pronoun
- using at least one possessive pronoun
- drawing on personal experience to support your comment.

'Being with friends is a major source of happiness.'
'Children who live in towns are happier than those who live in the countryside.'
'The sex of the child is also important – girls are often more unhappy than boys.'

Activity 11

Use your notes and your own knowledge and experience to write a magazine article called 'What makes children happy' for a parents' magazine. Your article should:

- inform parents in an interesting way about what makes children happy
- include comments
- be between 200 and 300 words long.

Follow steps 1–3.

Step 1: Selecting information

You do not have to use all of the information in your notes. Decide what your readers would find most interesting or surprising. Too many facts and figures can lose their impact, so use these sparingly. Look back over your notes and highlight the information you want to use. Jot down any other ideas about children's happiness based on your own experience.

Step 2: Ordering ideas

Use the sub-headings in your notes to help you decide the order for your article.
Think about:

- what your readers might want to hear about first
- the effect you want your article to have – do you want to shock your
  readers by explaining how many children are unhappy, or do you want
  to surprise them by telling them that children say money does not
  ensure happiness?

Step 3: Writing your article

Look back at the task. You have planned your article and are now ready to
write it. Remember to connect your ideas and comment on the results.

Connecting your ideas

Think about the words and phrases you might use to help you connect your
ideas. You will have used these many times before. Here are some reminders:

'It would seem that …'   'This suggests …'   'As earlier figures suggested …'
'It implies …'   'This is similar to …'   'Additionally …'

Commenting on the results

In order to make your article interesting for your readers, you should comment
on the results of the survey. Your comments will:

- help your readers to interpret the results more easily
- make your article more personal by including your views on the results.

Look back at the comments you wrote in Activity 9 and highlight any you
would like to include here. Jot down any other comments you want to include.

Feedback

When you have written your first draft, ask a partner to tick where they can see you have:
- gained the interest of your readers
- put your ideas into an order that is easy for the reader to follow
- linked your ideas using appropriate words and phrases
- included your own comments on the research findings in the reports.

Make improvements to your work following your partner's suggestions.

Completing an application form

So far, you have used your reading skills to make notes on the information in texts. Another test of your reading skills is completing application forms. You need to read carefully and make sure that you provide all of the right information in the correct places.

Activity 12

Read the following advertisement and the application form carefully. Either fill in a photocopy of the form or list the details you would need to include.

Sharpen punctuation

Using colons

A colon (:) is used to introduce lists or examples.

1 Find the place in the Island Watch advertisement where a colon is used to introduce a list.

2 Read the following sentences, putting a colon in the appropriate place.

- He enjoyed playing many sports cricket football basketball and squash.
- Macbeth is haunted by the image of Banquo's ghost 'Never shake thy gory locks at me.'
- I've always wanted to be an actor I have acted in four school plays and a pantomime.

Island Watch
Teenprog Productions

Have you got what it takes to live with a group of young people aged 13–16 on a tropical island for two weeks?

You will work together to provide your own food and shelter and carry out a series of challenges. All of this will be filmed for a TV programme – Island Watch – scheduled to be shown in the autumn.

The sort of person we are looking for is:

- outgoing and adventurous
- someone who enjoys a challenge
- a good team player.

If this sounds like you, Teenprog Productions would like to hear from you. Complete the application form and send it to:

**Tessa Longson,
Teenprog Productions,
Lockside, Stanton
ST14 6QP.
E-mail T.Longson@tpp.co.uk**

Teenprog Productions
Island Watch application

Please complete this section in black or blue ink, using block capitals.
Circle the location that would be most convenient for your interview.

London   Birmingham   Manchester   Bristol

A Personal details

First name _____   Home phone no. _____

Surname _____   Mobile phone no. _____

Date of birth _____   E-mail address _____

Gender _____

B Education

School attended _____   Favourite subjects _____

C Interests

What I would like to do when I leave school _____

Give Teenprog Productions a clear idea of who you are. Answer these questions.

- Favourite book?   • Greatest fear?
  _____   _____

- Favourite film?   • Greatest ambition?
  _____   _____

- Favourite song?   • Greatest achievement so far?
  _____   _____

- Dress style?
  _____   _____

D Friends & family

You will be on the island for two weeks without contact with family or friends.

- Which members of your family would you most miss and why? _____

  _____

- What (things) would you miss most and why? _____

  _____

E About you

- Have you got any bad habits? What are they? _____
- What's the nicest thing you have ever done? _____
- What makes you laugh? _____
- What makes you angry? _____

Signed ....

Date ....

Writing to persuade

Application forms often have a space for a **personal statement**. This is a longer piece of writing where you are asked to persuade the reader that you are a suitable candidate. You are going to write a personal statement of between 80–150 words to add to your application form for *Island Watch*. Your aim is to make the producers believe you have the right qualities and personality to take part.

Activity 13

1 The following are all features of persuasive writing:
   - persuasive language
   - use of humour
   - direct appeal to your readers
   - short sentences for emphasis
   - lively opening
   - convincing reasons
   - facts and evidence
   - language that appeals to feelings
   - snappy conclusion
   - organised detail.

   Which three do you think are most important in a personal statement?

2 With a partner, compare your choices. If you disagree on any of the features, explain your reasons for your choice.

You are now going to look at how you could use some of these when you write your personal statement.

Lively opening

It is important to make a good first impression on your reader. You need to begin with a powerful opening sentence that will grab the reader's attention.

Activity 14

1 Read the opening statements below. Place them in order according to the impact they have on you.
   A *Island Watch* sounds really good fun and I would love to be chosen to be part of the team.
   B Are you looking for an excellent team player with a great sense of humour, and a passion for the outdoors? Then look no further.
   C I've always wanted to be a TV star: I was an extra in *Hollyoaks* and have experience of appearing in several shows at school.
   D I'm an adventurous and outgoing person who relishes a challenge.

2 Write two opening statements that you could use in your personal statement.

3 Ask a partner to choose the one with the most impact. Try to improve it further.

Persuasive language

The words you choose need to make an impact on your readers. In your personal statement you should aim to emphasise your personality and qualities.

Activity 15

1 Look at the following statements. Decide which one has the most impact and why.

- I like to cook all different kinds of food.
- When it comes to cooking, I'm simply the best.
- Although I detest cooking, I'm a genius at washing up.

2 Write two statements about yourself. Aim to emphasise your personality and qualities.

Organised detail

It is very important to plan and think things through. In a personal statement you have a limited number of words, so you need to make every word count.

Snappy conclusion

Your final sentence is important. You need to leave your reader with a positive impression.

Activity 16

1 Put these final sentences in order with the most effective first. Explain your choices to a partner.

A I'm the person you're looking for: fun, outgoing and a great team player.

B For all of these reasons I believe I have a great deal to offer to the *Island Watch* team.

C *Island Watch* really appeals to me and I do hope I get chosen.

D Choose me: I make friends easily and I'm a budding TV star.

2 Write two final sentences that you could use in your personal statement. Aim to make a strong impression on your reader.

To do this you need to think about:

- who your reader is
- what you want to say
- the order in which you should place your ideas.

Activity 17

1 A student applying for a place on *Island Watch* has notes listed under the following headings. With a partner, talk about and decide on:

- which order they should place them in
- whether they should leave anything out.

a form representative on school council
b football team
c lively/sociable
d good team member
e willing to try new things/enjoy challenges
f technology favourite subject
g snorkelling/diving on holiday
h sensible/responsible
i please, please have me – final statement

2 List the different things you want to include in your personal statement. Place them in the order that would work best.

Writing your personal statement

Activity 18

1 Building on what you have learned so far, write the first draft of your personal statement. Remember to have:

- a lively opening
- organised detail
- persuasive language
- a snappy conclusion.

Your personal statement needs to be between 80–150 words.

2 When you have finished, ask a partner to read and comment on the impact of your personal statement. Make any improvements suggested by your partner and then write your final version.

Assessment task

CHOOSING THE RIGHT CANDIDATE

You work for a recruitment agency that assists companies in appointing the right staff. You have been asked to read three applications and make a presentation to your boss explaining why you would or would not wish to call each of the candidates for an interview. You will be assessed on your ability to:

- make notes on a range of texts
- discuss ideas in a group
- present your ideas.

Read this advertisement carefully.

STEEL ROW STUDIOS

Seeks an enthusiastic and committed individual to assist with all aspects of administrative and publicity work at these busy and successful studios.

You'll be involved in providing hospitality for visiting musicians and producers, providing administrative support for Bo Mellor, our director, and the production of marketing and publicity materials. Some international travel may be required.

You'll need education up to at least A-Level standard, excellent writing and IT skills, experience in a busy office environment and, of course, a keen interest in music.

Please apply in writing, explaining why you think you are suitable for this post and enclosing the names of two referees. Applications should be sent to:
Yolanda James, Steel Row Studios, Steel Row, London SW1 0DT by 30th January.

1 The agency has received more than 100 replies to this advertisement. In order to be able to choose the most suitable applicants, you need to have a thorough understanding of what the company wants. Re-read the advertisement and list the key skills and qualities required.

2 Read the three letters of application (pages 86–88), then copy and complete the table below.

	Applicant 1	Applicant 2	Applicant 3
Education			
Relevant work experience			
Personal qualities			

3 Basing your judgement on the notes you have just made, list the positive and negative qualities for each applicant.

4 Work in a group of three. Using the notes you have made summarise the suitability of each applicant and highlight any possible disadvantages. You should back up your recommendation with evidence, and you must reach agreement on the reasons for your recommendation.

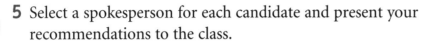

5 Select a spokesperson for each candidate and present your recommendations to the class.

Applicant 1: Suzy McLoughlin

94 Durnsbridge Street
Middlesbrough
TS3 2RT

Dear Ms James

I have recently read your advertisement for a general assistant at Steel Row Studios and would like to apply for this post.

At school I gained four 'A' Levels in English Language (grade B), ICT (grade B), Politics (grade A) and General Studies (grade C). At school I was considered to be very hardworking and conscientious. On leaving school I went to Sheffield University where I studied journalism. I graduated with a second class honours degree.

At university I played a full and active part in student life. I was a member of the very successful ladies' football team which I believe did a great deal to develop the qualities of responsibility, reliability and loyalty. I believe myself to be a very good team player who fits in well to any environment. I was also the music reporter for the student newspaper, which gave me the opportunity to attend many gigs, excellent preparation for the post of general assistant in a music studio.

Since leaving university I have been working as trainee for my local newspaper, the *Dukestown Echo*. My work involves shadowing a senior reporter, attending local events and writing reports for publications. This brings me into contact with a very wide range of people. I believe myself to be a very good communicator and particularly enjoy this aspect of my job. As a newspaper reporter I am a very confident user of IT.

I intend to relocate to London and to seek a change of direction in my career. I feel that I have many of the skills required as well as the relevant experience.

Yours sincerely

Suzy McLoughlin

Suzy Mcloughlin

Applicant 2: Adnan Amjad

Flat 3
22 Eversley Street
London
E5 9EH

Dear Ms James

With reference to your advertisement of 5th January for the post of assistant at Steele Row Studios, I would like to submit the following information.

First, I would like to inform you that I have a very keen interest in music and all aspects of the music business. I play the drums and the guitar, and I am a member of a successful band who play regularly in clubs. Recently, we were runners up in the Young and Gifted Rock and Roll competition, part of the London Life festival.

When I was at school I completed a work-experience placement at Devon Road Studios in Camden. My duties included meeting visiting musicians and providing refreshments for them, filing and organising promotional materials and observing the technicians at work, assisting wherever possible. I feel that this experience will be very valuable if I am successful in my application.

I left school two years ago with A levels in English Language (grade C) Music (grade A) and Business Studies (grade C). I chose not to go to university but instead to work abroad to gain experience in working with the public, as I am an outgoing friendly person and have always enjoyed working with people.

I spent eighteen months working in the Blue Sands Hotel in Jamaica. This was a small, but very busy hotel. As a result, I was able to gain much valuable experience in a variety of roles. I began by working as a waiter and then was promoted to post of assistant reception manager. My duties included supervising other workers and meeting the public and ensuring that their needs were met. I also dealt with correspondence and other aspects of hotel administration. I feel that many of the skills I acquired here could be put to good use at Steele Row Studios.

Since my return six months ago, I have worked as a temporary office assistant in a range of different offices across London. This has greatly enhanced my IT skills.

I am polite, hard working, lively and outgoing, and I feel that I would be an asset to Steele Row Studios.

Yours sincerely

Adnan Amjad

Adnan Amjad

Applicant 3: Liam Smithson

45 Lytholme Street
Crewe
CW4 5HN

Dear Ms James

I am writing in reply to the Steel Row Studios advertisement for a general assistant. First, I would like you to know that I am hard working, intelligent and passionate about music and performance. I am a very confident person who gets on well with a wide range of people. I very much enjoy working as part of a team and I feel that I have great deal to offer Steel Road Studios.

On leaving school with six GCSE's in Music, English, Drama, Maths, Technology and Science I spent two years working with my father as a general builder. This experience certainly taught me how to work very hard and especially how to get up in the morning! Throughout this time I was a singer and a songwriter with a successful band performing at venues across the north-west of England.

My experiences as a musician led me back to college where I enrolled for a BTEC National Diploma in Performing Arts. I studied drama, dance and music and gained Rock School grades in keyboard, vocals and guitar. After achieving four merits in my second year I then studied for an HND in Performing Arts at the University of Salford where I greatly developed my performance skills as well as following courses in production techniques and technologies.

Whilst a student at Salford, I was a member of a musical and theatre group which toured Eastern Europe putting on performances for students in universities. I was also fortunate enough to gain employment as an extra in a film about rock music in Manchester.

Throughout my years at college and university I have always had part-time jobs to finance my education. I feel this has given me a great deal of determination and enabled me to develop a great deal of resilience in pursuing my ambitions.

I have recently graduated from university and I am looking for a career in the music industry. I am a keen and willing learner who is ready to acquire new skills. I am sure that my enthusiasm, energy and capacity for very hard work would enable me to carry out the role of assistant at Steel Row Studios.

Yours sincerely

Liam Smithson

Liam Smithson

4 Cultures and contexts

The bigger picture

In this unit you will explore how writers of fiction draw on literary traditions and use their knowledge of different cultures to form a background for their writing. You will consider how writers present their ideas in different ways and you will write in detail about one short story. At the end of the unit you will study a short story on your own and answer questions on it.

WHAT? You will:
- consider how a writer uses a traditional form when writing a short story
- examine how writers present their ideas and important issues
- analyse what a writer shows you about a different culture
- develop your skills in writing a formal essay

HOW? by:
- identifying the similarities between a modern short story and a traditional tale
- comparing two short stories set in different cultures
- reading and discussing an extended short story
- writing about an aspect of a short story

WHY? because:
- understanding how writers draw on the past extends your understanding of their craft
- comparison helps you to identify similarities and differences
- close reading and discussion help you to develop understanding
- in exams you will be asked to answer questions on texts and develop your ideas in writing.

Writing traditions

Writing in the present is shaped and influenced by things that have been written in the past. Traditional tales were first passed on by word of mouth and then written down. One of the best-known collections of such tales is Grimm's Fairy Tales.

Written by the brothers Grimm in the early 1800s, this was a collection of Germanic folk tales. They show us things about the lives, values and morals of the people of that time. One of these tales is called 'Aschenputtel'. It was one of the forerunners to the modern 'Cinderella'.

The original tale tells of the harsh life led by a young girl whose mother has died and whose father has remarried. It shows a rough justice in which the brave and determined heroine is eventually united with her prince. Her stepsisters, however, are left maimed and blinded. Similar tales exist in many other cultures, including Chinese and Indian.

By the time Walt Disney made his famous film in 1949, Cinderella had become a much milder character and the story was less brutal. She sings and dreams her days away and is generally a helpless heroine. This suited those times when sweetness and obedience were considered to be desirable qualities in young girls. It is this version of the story that is best known today. Here is a reminder of the story of Cinderella:

In the following short story, 'Ashputtel: or The Mother's Ghost', the writer draws on ideas from this well-known tale.

Activity 1

Make a copy of the table below and use it as you read the story to help you identify and list the similarities and differences between Ashputtel and Cinderella.

Cinderella:	Ashputtel:
<ul><li>lives among the ashes and has to work hard</li><li>is very unhappy</li><li>has two ugly sisters and a wicked stepmother</li><li>has a fairy godmother</li><li>animals help her get to the ball</li><li>wears a beautiful dress to the ball</li><li>meets her prince</li><li>leaves a glass slipper behind</li><li>is found by the prince</li></ul>	

Ashputtel: or The Mother's Ghost

A burned child lived in the ashes. No, not really burned – more charred, a little bit charred, like a stick half-burned and picked off the fire; she looked like charcoal and ashes because she lived in the ashes since her mother died and the hot ashes burned her, so she was scabbed and scarred. The burned child

5 lived on the hearth, covered in ashes, as if she was still mourning.

After her mother died and was buried, her father forgot the mother and forgot the child and married the woman who used to rake the ashes, and that was why the child lived in the unraked ashes and there was nobody to brush her hair, so it stuck out like a mat, nor to wipe the dirt off her scabbed face and she

10 had no heart to do it for herself, but she raked the ashes and slept beside the little cat and got the burned bits from the bottom of the pot to eat, scraping them out, squatting on the floor, by herself in front of the fire, not as if she were human, because she was still mourning.

Her mother was dead and buried but still felt the perfect, exquisite pain of

15 love when she looked up through the earth and saw the burned child covered in ashes.

'Milk the cow, burned child, and bring back all the milk,' said the stepmother, who used to rake the ashes and milk the cow before, but now the burned child did all that.

20 The ghost of the mother went into the cow.

'Drink some milk and grow fat,' said the mother's ghost.

The burned child pulled on the udder and drank enough milk before she took the bucket back and nobody saw and time passed and she grew fat, she grew breasts, she grew up.

25   There was a man the stepmother wanted and she asked him into the kitchen to give him his dinner, but she let the burned child cook it, although the stepmother did all the cooking before. After the burned child cooked the dinner the stepmother sent her off to milk the cow.

    'I want that man for myself,' said the burned child to the cow.

30   The cow let down more milk, and more, and more, enough for the girl to have a drink and wash her face and wash her hands. When she washed her face, she washed the scabs off and now she was not burned at all, but the cow was empty.

    'You must give your own milk, next time,' said the ghost of the mother inside
35 the cow. 'You've milked me dry.'

    The little cat came by. The ghost of the mother went into the cat.

    'Your hair wants doing,' said the cat. 'Lie down.'

    The little cat unpicked her raggy lugs with its clever paws until the burned child's hair hung down nicely, but it had been so snagged and tangled that the
40 cat's claws were all pulled out before it was finished.

    'Comb your own hair, next time,' said the cat. 'You've taken my strength away, I can't do it again.'

    The burned child was clean and combed but stark naked. There was a bird sitting in the apple tree. The ghost of the mother left the cat and went into the
45 bird. The bird struck its own breast with its beak. Blood poured down onto the burned child under the tree. It ran over her shoulders and covered her front and back. She shouted out when it ran down her legs. When the bird had no more blood, the burned child got a red silk dress.

    'Bleed your own dress, next time,' said the bird. 'I'm through with all that.'

50   The burned child went into the kitchen to show herself to the man. She was not burned any more, but lovely. The man left off looking at the stepmother and looked at the girl.

    'Come home with me and let your stepmother stay and rake the ashes,' he said to her and off they went. He gave her a house and money. She did all right
55 for herself.

    'Now I can go to sleep,' said the ghost of the mother. 'Now everything is all right.'

by Angela Carter

Language and style

It is not just ideas that writers draw from the past. They may also use features of language and style. Answer the questions in Activity 2 to help you identify how the writer of 'Ashputtel' draws on the language and style of traditional fairy tales.

Activity 2

1 Fairy tales have a traditional opening and ending.
  a How do traditional fairy tales open and end?
  b How does 'Ashputtel' open?
  c In what way is the ending of 'Ashputtel' similar to the close of a traditional fairy tale?

2 In fairy tales, words and ideas are often repeated so that they are easy to remember.
  a What two words appear in the opening sentence and are repeated four more times in the first paragraph? What is the effect of this?
  b What is similar about the ending of the first and the second paragraphs?
  c What is similar about the start of the second and third paragraphs?

3 In fairy tales things often happen in threes. What three similar things happen in lines 20–49?

4 What similarities can you find in the words spoken by the animals?

5 Writers of fairy tales often use the sounds of words to appeal to their readers. How does the writer use the sounds of words to add interest in the following lines?
  The little cat unpicked her raggy lugs with its clever paws until the burned child's hair hung down nicely, but it had been so snagged and tangled that the cat's claws were all pulled out before it was finished.

6 Writers of fairy tales often use dark and gruesome images to interest and frighten children. Try to find any images in the story that might be described as dark and gruesome.

Sharpen spelling

The possessive apostrophe

We use an apostrophe plus s ('s) to show the possessive form, for example:

the ghost of the mother ➝ *the mother's ghost*

When the possessor is plural and already ends with an s we just add an apostrophe to the end of the word, for example:

the ghosts of the mothers ➝ *the mothers' ghosts*

Irregular plurals take an apostrophe + s, for example:

the hair of the children ➝ *the children's hair*

Write the correct possessive forms of the following:
1 the milk of the cow ➝
2 the hair of the child ➝
3 the claws of the cats ➝
4 the claws of the cat ➝
5 the milk of the cows ➝
6 the dress of the burned child ➝

Drawing on tradition to develop ideas

Angela Carter, the writer of 'Ashputtel: or The Mother's Ghost', wrote her version of the tale in 1987, 37 years after Walt Disney made *Cinderella*. She develops a different kind of heroine and other ideas.

Activity 3

1 With a partner, talk about:
- the ways in which Ashputtel is different from Cinderella
- how the story of 'Ashputtel' is more suited to modern times.

2 'Ashputtel: or The Mother's Ghost' is more than just a fairy story. Make notes on the ways in which it is also about:
- cruelty to children
- revenge
- a mother's love.

3 Share your ideas with a partner or group and add to or change your notes in the light of your discussion.

Developing ideas in paragraphs

Paragraphs can be developed in different ways. In the following paragraph, the writer focuses on the child and builds up detail about her in one long extended sentence. She keeps the focus on the child, partly by the use of pronouns. The first five references to the child are highlighted for you. Pick out and list the other seven pronouns used in the paragraph.

After her mother died and was buried, her father forgot the mother and forgot the child and married the woman who used to rake the ashes, and that was why the child lived in the unraked ashes and there was nobody to brush her hair, so it stuck out like a mat, nor to wipe the dirt off her scabbed face and she had no heart to do it for herself, but she raked the ashes and slept beside the little cat and got the burned bits from the bottom of the pot to eat, scraping them out, squatting on the floor, by herself in front of the fire, not as if she were human, because she was still mourning.

Sharpen punctuation

Quotation marks

Quotation marks can be used: in a handwritten text, whenever you refer to the title of a book, magazine, film, photograph, game or similar thing, for example: She notices the photograph under the heading 'Drought in Africa'.

Rewrite the following paragraph from the story 'The Photograph' (pages 98–9), using quotation marks where appropriate:

The story, The Photograph, is about two girls from two very different continents. It shows how one girl is so desperate to be on the cover of Vogue that she fails to see how the other girl is starving. If I were to base a film on this story it would be called The Two Faces of Africa.

In the next paragraph the writer writes about three different things: the burned child, the bird and the blood. The use of a series of short sentences helps to develop the ideas without confusing the reader. The references to the burned child are highlighted for you. Copy the paragraph and highlight, using different colours, the references to the bird and the blood.

> The burned child was clean and combed but stark naked. There was a bird sitting in the apple tree. The ghost of the mother left the cat and went into the bird. The bird struck its own breast with its beak. Blood poured down onto the burned child under the tree. It ran over her shoulders and covered her front and back. She shouted out when it ran down her legs. When the bird had no more blood, the burned child got a red silk dress.

Activity 4

You are going to write two paragraphs, using the example paragraphs as models. Choose a character from a traditional or modern fairy tale, such as the wolf in 'Little Red Riding Hood', the prince in *The Little Mermaid*, the donkey in *Shrek*.

Paragraph 1 – Aim to:
- give details about where your character lives and what they are like
- write one extended sentence to help keep the focus on your character
- use pronouns to help keep the focus on the character.

Paragraph 2 – Aim to:
- keep your main character and introduce another
- recount something that happens between them
- write five or six sentences to help you develop ideas without confusing the reader.

 **Highlight thinking**

Application means trying out new ideas in your own work. It is an important stage in your thinking and learning. When you have understood a new idea or way of going about things, you should try it out in your own work. After you have used the new ideas, you will be ready to evaluate them and decide how well they have worked.

 Feedback

Read through the paragraphs you have written and check them as follows.
1 Highlight, using one colour, the words that keep the focus on the character in Paragraph 1.
2 Highlight, using two colours, the references to the two characters in Paragraph 2.
3 Check that you have written one extended sentence in Paragraph 1 and five or six sentences in Paragraph 2.
4 Compare your paragraphs with a partner's.
5 Make any improvements that you feel are needed before moving on.

Writing from different cultures

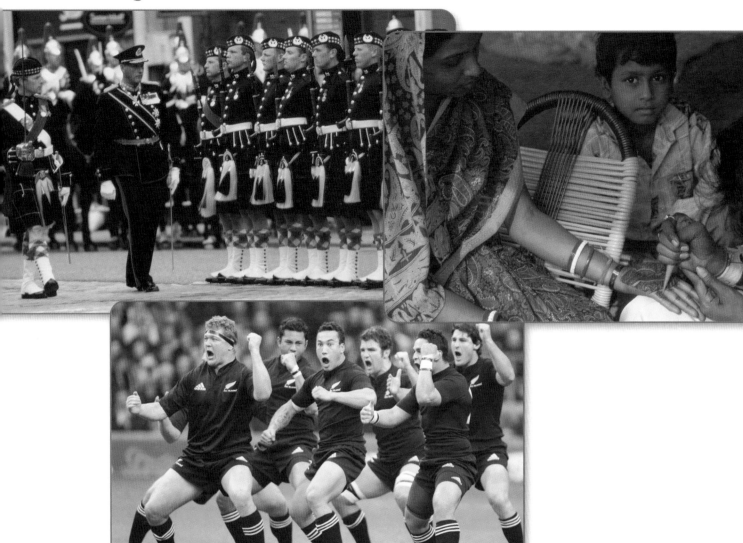

The word 'culture' is a general term for the huge range of ideas, knowledge and beliefs that are generally shared by the people of a country, religion or ethnic or social group. Many people draw on a number of different cultures based on their family background or life experience. In pairs or groups:

- list the different cultures you know something about
- talk about the different cultures that play a part in your lives.

The following story, 'The Photograph', is written by Sefi Atta. She was born in Nigeria, Africa, was educated in England and later studied in America.

Activity 5

When you have read the story, make notes on what you are shown about:

- life in Africa
- life in America.

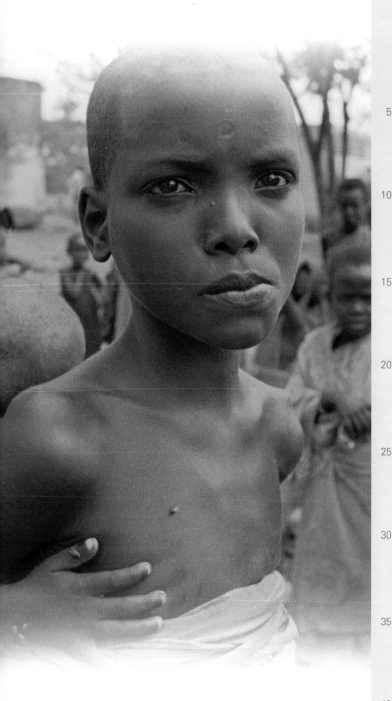

The Photograph

Picture her: a girl with hollow cheeks and
sunken eyes; her dress hangs off her shoulders.
Dust spirals above her in the aftermath of the
relief trucks. Their huge tyre marks on the dry
5 ground are all that's left of the mission to her
village. The sun is at its hottest; the African sky
endless and merciless. Even the white men with
cameras, clicking away to capture the usual
scrimmage over food deliveries, are hopping
10 into their jeeps, and speeding off to an air-
conditioned hotel in a city miles away. They are
photojournalists.

One of them, sun-burned and drenched in
sweat, dressed in a khaki shirt and jeans, kneels
15 to take a photograph of the girl before he
leaves. In his breast pocket is a melted protein
bar, as untouched as his conscience. He is not
responsible for the cruelty of nature, or the
incompetence of governments. And who really
20 can tolerate the stench of human waste in a
ditch nearby, unless they have no choice but to
live in a place like this?

Professionally, the girl caught his attention.
She was surrounded by a group of boys, and
25 she seemed just as determined as they
scrambled when the relief trucks arrived. She
was pushed down and trampled on. When she
found her feet, the sacks of grain had already
been dragged away. She remained there, red-
30 eyed, and stroking the earth with her fingertips.

The journalist takes his final shot, returns to
America with several reels of film. His
photograph of the girl sells and is placed on the
front cover of a magazine for current affairs. He
35 receives accolades and gains enemies among
his colleagues. He changes his girlfriend for one
who thinks he is under-appreciated and cavalier.
'You've captured the face of hunger in Africa,'
his editor summarises about the photograph,
40 and he stops himself from reminding the man
that this photograph is just one face, in one

village in Africa. Still, he benefits from the praise, and the recognition for his work, at last.

45 The photograph is in most news-stands by month end, even in the bookstore of a mall in America that people visit to peruse bestsellers and magazines with no intention of buying them. They look at the face of the African girl and quickly turn away to salvage their shopping
50 sprees. But they are struck by her image, like one teenager who has finished flipping through the latest copy of *Vogue*. She notices the photograph under the heading 'Drought in Africa'. Her parents are from that continent. She
55 herself was born and bred in America, raised on Disney and has never travelled out. She is embarrassed by such images. They remind her of her classmates who joke about starving Africans. She isn't African that way, or American
60 in an apple pie way either.

When she was a girl, Cinderella, Snow White and all the other Disney princesses didn't resemble her. When she became interested in fashion, neither did the cover models. Then, it
65 seemed the magazines discovered Africa had beautiful women. There was the model from Sudan who, supposedly, was once a refugee; there was the Nigerian model who was discovered in the Miss Africa pageant.

70 This Nigerian model is in the latest copy of *Vogue*, dressed in linen, and thin, so thin the teenager is conscious of her own hips. She thinks she is too fat. She wants to wear jeans that cling to her bones like skin. She would love
75 to be photographed with aloof eyes like the Nigerian model. She diets on protein shakes and secretly sticks her finger down her throat to vomit. And it doesn't matter what reasons there are for a world where some people starve, while
80 others starve themselves. The hunger that consumes her is real, so she stares at the girl in the photograph, ignores the background of drought, and admires her cheekbones.

by Sefi Atta

The writer's point of view

Sometimes writers show you things in a new or different light, perhaps in a way you hadn't thought of before. The questions in Activity 6 will help you to explore the writer's point of view in 'The Photograph'.

Activity 6

Lines 1–12

1 The story starts with the command 'Picture her'. What words does the writer use to show the poor physical health of the girl? How do you think the writer wants the reader to react to this description?

2 What two adjectives are used to describe the African sky? What do these words suggest to you?

3 The photojournalists are referred to as 'the white men'. Why does the writer mention their colour?

4 How does the writer emphasise the contrast between the lives of the photojournalists and of the people they are photographing?

Lines 13–30

5 What different things are suggested by the line: 'In his breast pocket is a melted protein bar, as untouched as his conscience'?

6 How is the girl presented as being both plucky and vulnerable?

Lines 31–43

7 Re-read these lines closely. What is the writer's opinion of the photographer? What makes you think this?

Lines 44–60

8 Why do the shoppers 'quickly turn away' after looking at the face of the girl?

9 What is it about the image that embarrasses the second girl?

10 'She isn't African that way, or American in an apple pie way either.' Explain what you think these lines mean.

Lines 61–83

11 How does the girl want to look and what does she do to try to achieve this?

12 What point do you think the writer is trying to emphasise by comparing the two girls in this way?

Putting your ideas together

13 Using the notes you made when reading the story and your answers to questions 1–12, write three paragraphs explaining:
   • what the writer shows you about life in Africa
   • what the writer shows you about life in America
   • the connections the writer makes between the two places.

Using evidence from a text

When you write about a text, you should refer to evidence in it to support the points you make. This evidence may be details from the text, for example:

We suspect the photojournalist does not care about the hungry people as he has kept the melted protein bar in his pocket.

Sometimes you need to quote directly from the text as evidence. You might quote single words or phrases, for example:

We realise that the famine in Africa is not bad news for everyone as the photojournalist 'benefits from the praise, and the recognition for his work'.

Notice how quotation marks are placed directly before and after the words taken from the text.

Occasionally, you might quote a whole sentence or more as evidence, for example:

It is clear that the second girl has an obsession with her weight as: 'She diets on protein shakes and secretly sticks her finger down her throat to vomit.'

Notice how a colon (:) is used to show that the quotation is to follow.

Sharpen spelling

The apostrophe for omission

We use an apostrophe to shorten two words into one, for example:

that is	→ that's	you have	→ you've
is not	→ isn't	did not	→ didn't

Note that the apostrophe is put in the place of the missing letter or letters. In each of the following sentences, two words can be shortened into one. Rewrite the sentences using apostrophes. The first one has been done for you.

1 The sun is at its hottest. → The sun's at its hottest.
2 They are photojournalists.
3 He is not responsible for the cruelty of nature.
4 This photograph is just one face, in one village in Africa.
5 But they are struck by her image.
6 She would love to be photographed.

Activity 7

1 Copy and complete the following sentences using suitable words or phrases from 'The Photograph'. Remember to use quotation marks.

   a The writer shows how hot the sun is when she describes the African sky as being _____'.

   b The girl was unable to get to the sacks of grain because she was '_____'.

   c When the photojournalist returns to America his photograph is seen by many because it _____.

   d The editor believes the photograph captures _____.

2 Copy and complete the following paragraph by adding colons and quotation marks. Highlight the punctuation you have added.

> The girl in America is clearly unsure about her identity as we are told that she isn't African that way, or American in an apple pie way either. She believes that to succeed she needs to be very thin. She wants to wear jeans that cling to her bones like skin.

Linking paragraphs

'The Photograph' is a tightly structured story. The opening paragraph introduces both the girl and the photojournalists. Pronouns are used to keep the focus, first on the girl and then on the photojournalists. Some detail is given to describe the setting. Different colours are used to highlight the details connected with the girl, photojournalist and the setting.

Picture her: a girl with hollow cheeks and sunken eyes; her dress hangs off her shoulders. Dust spirals above her in the aftermath of the relief trucks. Their huge tyre marks on the dry ground are all that's left of the mission to her village. The sun is at its hottest; the African sky endless and merciless. Even the white men with cameras, clicking away to capture the usual scrimmage over food deliveries, are hopping into their jeeps, and speeding off to an air-conditioned hotel in a city miles away. They are photojournalists.

 Activity 8

1 Trace the connected details in lines 13–23 relating to:
  * the photograph
  * the people
  * one teenager.

Either copy and highlight the paragraph and highlight the connected details in different colours, or list the connected details.

2 The paragraphs in this story are closely linked by the opening and closing sentences. The table shows how this is done. Study the table closely and continue it showing the links between the closing and opening sentences of the fourth, fifth, sixth and seventh paragraphs of the story.

Paragraphs	Opening/closing sentences	Link
Para 1 ends with:	They are photojournalists.	
Para 2 opens with:	One of them, sun-burned and drenched in sweat, dressed in a khaki shirt and jeans, kneels to take a photograph of the girl before he leaves.	The reader is moved on from the group of journalists to one in particular, but the focus on the girl is maintained.
Para 2 ends with:	And who really can tolerate the stench of human waste in a ditch nearby, unless they have no choice but to live in a place like this?	This shows the photojournalist's lack of feeling for the poor people.
Para 3 opens with:	Professionally, the girl caught his attention.	The word 'professionally' emphasises that it is his job only and that his feelings are not engaged.
Para 3 ends with:	She remained there, red-eyed, and stroking the earth with her fingertips.	The focus is back on the girl who must stay in this place.
Para 4 opens with:	The journalist takes his final shot, returns to America with several reels of film.	The final shot is of the girl as she was at the end of the third paragraph. The girl stays, but in contrast the journalist 'returns to America'.

Feedback

Share your answers to Activity 8 with a partner. Check that you had:

- the same details highlighted in response to question 1
- similar ideas on the links between the opening and closing sentences in response to question 2.

Where there are differences, talk about them and amend your answers if necessary.

✓ Progress check

So far in this unit you have read two short stories. You have learnt about:

- how 'Ashputtel' draws on the literary tradition of the fairy tale
- how 'The Photograph' shows us things about different cultures
- what the writers might be trying to say through their stories
- how to refer to the text when writing about a story.

You are now going to test a partner on how well they have learnt these things.

1 Write four questions, one for each of the points listed above. Your aim is to check your partner's learning.
2 Make a separate note of the answers you expect your partner to give.
3 Exchange questions and write the answers to your partner's questions.
4 Compare their answers with the answers you expected and talk about any differences.

Comparing texts

When you compare two texts you look for the similarities and differences between them. To do this you need to consider:

- what the stories are about
- the ways the ideas are presented in the stories.

Activity 9

Work in small groups. You are going to discuss and make notes on the similarities and differences between 'Ashputtel: or The Mother's Ghost' and 'The Photograph'. You will need a large piece of paper.

1 As a group, decide on the following.

- **How** you are going to record the points you make in discussion. These notes will need to be clear enough for other people to follow.
- **Who** is going to record them.

2 Talk about the following to help you make notes on the similarities and differences between the stories. You could start by thinking about:

- the main characters
- the writers' points of view
- the settings
- the openings and endings
- your responses to the two stories.

- what happens in the stories
- the cultures or traditions in the stories.
- the ways the stories are written
- ideas that occur in both stories

3 Find and make notes of evidence in the stories to support your points. **Either** contribute your notes to a class display **or** take it in turns for each group to explain their notes to the class.

Writing about a short story

You are now going to read and make notes on a story from a different culture. 'A Drink of Water' is by Samuel Selvon, a writer from Trinidad in the West Indies. You will then write a detailed essay in answer to the question: **What does the writer show us about the people who live in Las Lomas in 'A Drink of Water'?**

Making notes

Your notes are for your use. They need to be sufficiently clear and detailed for you to make use of them later.

You can use spider diagrams, tables, bulleted lists or any other helpful form of recording information.

You can use initials for names, for example in your notes on this story you could write 'M.' for Manko, 'R.' for Rampersad, 'L.L.' for Las Lomas. You do not need to write in sentences and you can use symbols and abbreviations, for example:

∴ = 'therefore'   i.e. = 'that is'
∵ = 'because'   e.g. = 'for example'
> = 'more than'   re. = 'relating to'

Understanding the text

Activity 10

Read the story closely and aim to gain a good understanding of the setting, the plot and the characters. To help you do this, talk about questions 1–9 as you read the story. Make notes on your answers, either while you are reading the story or when you have read it.

A Drink of Water

The time when the rains didn't come for three months and the sun was a yellow furnace in the sky was known as the Great Drought in Trinidad. It happened when everyone was expecting the sky to burst open with rain to fill the dry streams and water the parched earth.

5 But each day was the same; the sun rose early in a blue sky, and all day long the farmers lifted their eyes, wondering what had happened to Parjanya, the rain god. They rested on their hoes and forks and wrung perspiration from their clothes, seeing no hope in labour, terrified by the thought that if no rain fell soon they would lose their crops and livestock and face starvation and death.

10 In the tiny village of Las Lomas, out in his vegetable garden, Manko licked dry lips and passed a wet sleeve over his dripping face. Somewhere in the field a cow mooed mournfully, sniffing around for a bit of green in the cracked earth. The field was a desolation of drought. The trees were naked and barks peeled off trunks as if they were diseased. When the wind blew, it was heavy and
15 unrelieving, as if the heat had taken all the spirit out of it. But Manko still opened his shirt and turned his chest to it when it passed.

He was a big man, grown brown and burnt from years of working on the land. His arms were bent and he had a crouching position even when he stood upright. When he laughed he showed more tobacco stain than teeth.

20 But Manko had not laughed for a long time. Bush fires had swept Las Lomas and left the garden plots charred and smoking. Cattle were dropping dead in the heat. There was scarcely any water in the village; the river was dry with scummy mud. But with patience one could collect a bucket of water. Boiled, with a little sugar to make it drinkable, it had to do.

25 Sometimes, when the children knew that someone had gone to the river for water, they hung about in the village main road waiting with bottles and calabash shells, and they fell upon the water-carrier as soon as he hove in sight.

'Boil the water first before drinking!' was the warning cry. But even so two children were dead and many more were on the sick list, their parents too poor
30 to seek medical aid in the city twenty miles away.

Manko sat in the shade of a mango tree and tried to look on the bright side of things. Such a dry season meant that the land would be good for corn seeds when the rain came. He and his wife Rannie had been working hard and saving money with the hope of sending Sunny, their son, to college in the city.

35 Rannie told Manko: 'We poor, and we ain't have no education, but is all right, we go get old soon and dead, and what we have to think about is the boy. We must let him have plenty learning and come a big man in Trinidad.'

1 Read lines 1–30. What do you learn about the place and the people who live there?

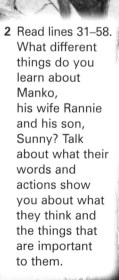

2 Read lines 31–58. What different things do you learn about Manko, his wife Rannie and his son, Sunny? Talk about what their words and actions show you about what they think and the things that are important to them.

And Manko, proud of his son, used to boast in the evening, when the villagers got together to talk and smoke, that one day Sunny would be a lawyer
40 or a doctor.

But optimism was difficut now. His livestock was dying out, and the market was glutted with yams. He had a great pile in the yard which he could not sell.

Manko took a look at his plot of land and shook his head. There was no sense in working any more today. He took his cutlass and hoe and calabash
45 shell which had a string so he could hold it dangling. He shook it, and realised with burning in his throat that it was empty, though he had left a few mouthfuls in it. He was a fool; he should have known that the heat would dry it up if he took it out in the garden with him. He licked his lips and, shouldering the tools, walked slowly down the winding path which led to his hut.

50 Rannie was cooling in the open fireplace in the yard. Sunny was sitting under the **poui tree**, but when he saw his father he ran towards him and held the calabash shell eagerly. Always when Manko returned from the fields he brought back a little water for his son. But this time he could only shake his head.

'Who went for water today by the river?' he asked Rannie.

55 'I think was Jagroop,' she answered, stirring the pot with a large wooden spoon, 'but he ain't coming back till late.'

She covered the pot and turned to him. 'Tomorrow we going to make offering for rain,' she said.

Next day, Las Lomas held a big feast, and prayers were said to the rain god,
60 Parjanya. And then two days later, a man called Rampersad struck water in a well he had been digging for weeks. It was the miracle they had been praying for. That day everyone drank their fill, and Rampersad allowed each villager a bucket of water, and Manko told Sunny: 'See how blessing doesn't only come from up the sky, it does come from the earth, too.'

65 Rampersad's wife was a selfish and crafty woman, and while the villagers were filling their buckets she stood by the doorway of their hut and watched them. That night she told her husband he was a fool to let them have the water for nothing.

'They have money hide up,' she urged him. 'They could well pay for it. The
70 best thing to do is to put barb' wire all round the well, and set a watchdog to keep guard in the night so nobody thief the water. Then say you too poor to give away for nothing. Charge a dollar for a bucket and two shillings for half-bucket. We make plenty money and come rich.'

3 Read lines 59–79. How and why do Rampersad's actions change in these lines?

Word bank

poui tree a pink and yellow tree which is the national tree of Trinindad
bap father

When Rampersad announced this, the villagers were silent and aghast that a
man could think of such a scheme when the whole village was burning away in
the drought, and two children had died.

Rampersad bought a shotgun and said he would shoot anyone he found
trespassing on his property. He put up the barbed wire and left a ferocious
watchdog near the well at nights.

As April went, there was still no sign in the sky. In Las Lomas, the villagers
exhausted their savings in buying Rampersad's water to keep alive.

Manko got up one morning and looked in the tin under his bed in which he
kept his money. There was enough for just two buckets of water. He said to
Rannie: 'How long could you make two buckets of water last, if we use it only
for drinking?'

'That is all the money remaining?' Rannie looked at him with fear.

He nodded and looked outside where the poui tree had begun to blossom. 'Is
a long time now,' he said softly, 'a long time, too long. It can't last. The rain will
fall, just don't be impatient.'

Rannie was not impatient, but thirst made her careless. It happened soon
after the two buckets were empty. She forgot to boil a pan of river water, and
only after she had drunk a cupful did she realise her fatal mistake. She was
afraid to tell Manko; she kept silent about the incident.

Next day, she could not get out of bed. She rolled and tossed as fever
ravaged her body.

Manko's eyes were wide with fright when he saw the signs of fever. Sunny,
who had not been to school for weeks, wanted to do whatever he could,
anything at all, to get his mother well so she could talk and laugh and cook
again.

He spoke to his father after Rannie had fallen into a fitful sleep, with
perspiration soaking though the thin white sheet.

'No money remaining for water, **bap**?'

Manko shook his head.

'And no money for doctor or medicine?'

He shook his head again.

'But how it is this man Rampersad have so much water and we ain't have
any? Why don't we just go and take it?'

'The water belong to Rampersad,' Manko said. 'Is his own, and if he choose
to sell it, is his business. We can't just go and take it, that would be thiefing.
You must never thief from another man, Sunny. That is a big, big, sin. No matter
what happen.'

75
80
85
90
95
100
105
110

4 Read lines
80–118. Imagine
you are Sunny.
What different
kinds of things
might you be
thinking about:
• Rampersad
• your mother,
  Rannie
• your father,
  Manko?

'But is not a fair thing,' the boy protested, digging his hands into the brittle soil. 'If we had clean water, we could get **mai** better, not so?'

'Yes, **beta**,' Manko sighed and rose to his feet. 'You stay and mind *mai*, I

115 going to try and get some river water.'

All day, Sunny sat in the hut brooding over the matter, trying hard to understand why his mother should die from lack of water when a well was filled in another man's yard.

It was late in the evening when Manko returned. As he had expected, the river

120 was nearly dry, a foul trickle of mud not worth drinking. He found the boy quiet and moody. After a while, Sunny went out.

Manko was glad to be alone. He didn't want Sunny to see him leaving the hut later in the night, with the bucket and the rope. It would be difficult to explain that he was stealing Rampersad's water only because it was a matter of life or

125 death.

He waited impatiently for Rannie to fall asleep. It seemed she would never close her eyes. She just turned and twisted restlessly, and once she looked at him and asked if rain had fallen, and he put his rough hand on her hot forehead and said softly no, but that he had seen a sign that evening, a great black cloud

130 low down in the east.

Then suddenly her fever rose again, and she was delirious. This time he could not understand what she said. She was moaning in a queer, strangled way.

It was midnight before she fell into a kind of swoon, a red flush on her face. Manko knew what he must do now. He stood looking at her, torn between the

135 fear of leaving her and the desperate plan that he had made. She might die while he was gone, and yet – he must try it.

He frowned as he went out and saw the moon like a night sun in the sky, lighting up the village. He turned to the east and his heart leapt as he saw the cloud moving towards the village in a slow breeze. It seemed so far away, and it

140 was moving as if it would take days to get over the fields. Perhaps it would; perhaps it would change direction and go scudding down into the west, and not a drop of water.

He moved off towards the well, keeping behind the huts and deep into the trees. It took him ten minutes to get near the barbed wire fence, and he stood in

145 the shadow of a giant silk-cotton tree. He leaned against the trunk and drew in his breath sharply as his eyes discerned a figure on the other side of the well, outside the barbed wire.

Word bank

mai mother
beta child

5 Read lines 119–49. In what different ways does the writer show us that Manko is under a great deal of pressure?

6 As we read stories we often predict what will happen next, based on stories we already know and on clues given to us by the writer. Before you read lines 150–208, write down your prediction and your reasons for it.

The figure stopped, as though listening, then began clambering over the fence.

150 Even as he peered to see if he could recognise who it was, a sudden darkness fell as the cloud swept over the moon in the freshening wind.

Manko cast his eyes upwards swiftly, and when he looked down again the figure was on the brink of the well, away from the sleeping watchdog.

It was a great risk to take; it was the risk Manko himself had to take. But this
155 intrusion upset his plan. He could not call out; the slightest sound would wake the dog, and what it did not do to the thief, Rampersad would do with his shotgun.

For a moment, Manko's heart failed him. He smelt death very near – for the unknown figure at the well, and for himself, too. He had been a fool to come.
160 Then a new frenzy seized him. He remembered the cruel red flush on Rannie's cheeks when he had left her. Let her die happy, if a drop of water could make her so. Let her live, if a drop of water could save her. His own thirst flared in his throat; how much more she must be suffering!

He saw the bucket slide noiselessly down and the rope paid out. Just what
165 he had planned to do. Now draw it up, cautiously, yes, and put it to rest gently on the ground. Now kneel and take a drink, and put the fire out in your body. For God's sake, why didn't the man take a drink? What was he waiting for? Ah, that was it, but be careful, do not make the slightest noise, or everything will be ruined. Bend your head down …

170 Moonrays shot through a break in the cloud and lit up the scene.

It was Sunny.

'*Beta!*' Before he could think, the startled cry had left Manko's lips.

The dog sprang up at the sound and moved with uncanny swiftness. Before Sunny could turn, it had sprung across the well, straight at the boy's throat.

175 Manko scrambled over the fence, ripping away his clothes and drawing blood. He ran and cleared the well in a great jump, and tried to tear the beast away from the struggling boy. The dog turned, growling low in the throat as it faced this new attacker.

Manko stumbled and fell, breathing heavily. He felt teeth sink into his
180 shoulder and he bit his lip hard to keep from screaming in pain.

Suddenly the dog was wrenched away as Sunny joined the fight. The boy put his arms around the dog's neck and jerked it away from his father with such force that when the animal let go they both fell rolling to the ground.

Manko flung out his arm as he sprang up. In doing so, he capsized the bucket
185 of water with a loud clang. Even in the struggle for life he could not bear to see the earth sucking up the water like a sponge. In fear and fury, he snatched the empty bucket and brought it down with all his strength on the dog's head.

The animal gave a whimper and rolled off the boy and lay still.

'Who's that, thiefing my water?' Rampersad came running out into the yard,
190 firing his shotgun wildly in the air.

'Quick, boy! Over the fence!' Manko grabbed the bucket and tossed it over. He almost threw Sunny to safety as the boy faltered on the wire. Then he half-dragged his own bleeding body up, and fell exhausted on the other side.

Sunny put his arm under his father and helped him up. Together they ran into
195 the shadow of the trees.

The noise of the gun and Rampersad's yells had wakened the whole village, and everyone was astir.

Father and son hid the bucket in a clump of dry bush and, waiting for a minute to recover themselves, joined the crowd which was gathering in front of
200 Rampersad's hut.

Rampersad was beside himself with rage. He threatened them all with jail, screaming that he would find out who had stolen the water and killed the dog.

'Who is the thief? You catch him?' the crowd jeered and booed. 'It damn good. Serve you right.' Clutching his father's arm tightly, Sunny danced and
205 chuckled with delight at Rampersad's discomfiture.

But suddenly silence and darkness fell together. A large black blob of cloud blotted out the moon. The sky was thick with clouds piling up on each other and there was a new coolness in the wind.

As one, the crowd knelt and prayed to the rain god. The sky grew black; it
210 looked as if the moon had never been there. For hours they prayed, until Manko, thinking of Rannie, gently tapped his son and beckoned him away. They walked home hand in hand.

It was Sunny who felt the first drop. It lay on his hand like a diamond shining in the dark.

215 '*Bap*?' He raised questioning eyes to his father. 'Look!'

7 How close were you in your prediction? Talk about the things you got right and how you had worked them out. Did anything happen that you had not predicted? What?

8 Talk about the different ways the writer could choose to end this story. Which way do you think would be the best? Now read lines 209–249. How good an ending do you think this is? Give your reasons.

As Manko looked up, another drop fell on his face and rolled down his cheek. The wind became stronger; there was a swift fall of some heavy drops. Then the wind died with a sigh. A low rumble in the east; then silence. Perhaps Parjanya was having a joke with them, perhaps there would be no rain after all.

220 And then it came sweeping in from the north-east, with a rising wind. Not very heavy at first, but in thrusts, coming and going. They opened their mouths and laughed, and water fell in. They shouted and cried and laughed again.

Manko approached the hut where Rannie lay, and he was trembling at what he would find. He said to the boy: '*Beta*. You stay here. I go in first to see *mai*.'
225 The boy's face went rigid with sudden fear. Though he was already drenched to the skin, he took shelter under the poui tree in the yard.

Manko was hardly inside the door when he gave a sharp cry of alarm. He thought he saw a ghostly figure tottering towards him, its face luminous-grey. He flattened himself against the wall and closed his eyes. It was cruel of the
230 gods to torment him like this. This was not Rannie: Rannie was lying in bed in the next room, she could not be alive any more.

'Manko.' It was her voice, and yet it was not her voice. 'What noise is that I hear? Is rain?'

He could not speak. Slowly, he forced himself to stretch out his hand and
235 touch her forehead. It felt cold and unnatural.

He withdrew his hand, and began to tremble uncontrollably.

'Manko,' the lips formed the words. 'Manko, give me water!'

Something fell to the floor with a clatter. He saw that it was a tin cup and that she had been holding it in her hand. She swayed towards him, and he caught her.
240 Then Manko knew that it was a miracle. Rannie was shaking with cold and weakness, but the fever was gone, and she was alive.

Realisation burst upon him with such force that he almost fainted.

He muttered: 'I will get some for you.'

He picked up the cup and ran out into the lashing rain. Sunny, watching from
245 the poui tree, was astonished to see his father standing motionless in the downpour. He had taken off his shirt, and his bare back and chest were shining with water. His face, uplifted to the sky, was the face of a man half-crazy with joy. He might be laughing or crying, Sunny could not tell; and his cheeks were streaming, perhaps with tears, perhaps with Parjanya's rain.

by Samuel Selvon

9 Think back over the whole story. What evidence can you find to suggest that the people in Las Lomas:
• lack technology
• are religious
• are caring?

Thinking about the issues

You now need to think more closely about some of the issues raised by the writer.

Activity 11

Role play

A range of attitudes are represented in the story.

C 'But it is not a fair thing,' the boy protested … 'If we had clean water, we could get *mai* better …'

E Rampersad … threatened them all with jail, screaming that he would find out who had stolen the water and killed the dog.

A The villagers were silent and aghast that a man could think of such a scheme …

B 'The water belong to Rampersad,' Manko said. … You must never thief from another man, Sunny. That is a big, big, sin. No matter what happen.'

D It would be difficult to explain that he was stealing Rampersad's water only because it was a matter of life or death.

F 'Who is the thief? You catch him?' the crowd jeered and booed. 'It damn good. Serve you right.'

1 Work in groups of four. You are going to role play the following characters. Decide who is going to play:
- Manko
- Sunny
- Rampersad
- a villager.

2 In role, work out what your character would feel and say about:
- the drought
- the raiding of the well
- Rampersad's actions
- the arrival of rain.

3 Imagine that the four characters meet in the village square. Rampersad has lost his money, his wife has left him and he needs help to dig a new well.
- Talk about how the situation might develop.
- Have a go at acting it out, making it up as you go along. This type of role play is called *improvisation*.
- Your improvisation should last for two to three minutes.

> ### Sharpen punctuation
>
> **The semi-colon**
> A semi-colon is stronger than a comma but not as strong as a full stop. It is used when two ideas are so closely linked that they ought to stay together, for example:
>
> *There was scarcely any water in the village; the river was dry with scummy mud.*
>
> Find and copy **four** other examples of the use of semi-colons in the story 'A Drink of Water'. Explain why each semi-colon has been used.

4 Now work out of role and share your ideas on the following questions.
- What do you think of the way Rampersad behaved in the story?
- Manko told Sunny it was a sin to steal but then he went on to try to steal water. What do you think about the way Manko behaved in the story?

5 Talk about other situations you can think of where it might seem 'right' to do something 'wrong', perhaps to help a friend or to avoid making a situation worse?

Organising your writing

You are now ready to start to plan your answer to the question: **What does the writer show us about the people who live in Las Lomas in 'A Drink of Water'?**

 Activity 12
Follow steps 1–7.

Step 1: gather ideas
Use your notes to help you gather your ideas about the people in Las Lomas. You could set out your ideas in a spider diagram like this.

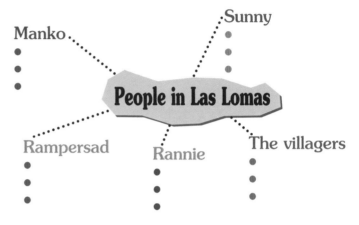

Step 2: plan your answer
Decide an order for your writing.
You could follow this order:
- what life is like for the people
- what is shown about the villagers
- what is shown about Manko
- what is shown about Sunny and Rannie
- what is shown about Rampersad
- what the writer shows about right and wrong.

These bullet points could form the basis of six paragraphs.

Step 3: find supporting evidence
Skim-read the story to find and list:
- things to refer to in your answer
- words to use in quotations.

Step 4: write your introduction
Your introduction should link directly to the task. Aim to:
- name the story and the writer and say where the story is set
- say that the story is about a number of different people
- briefly describe what life is like for these people
- say that the writer shows us about people through their actions, their words and what other people say about them.

Step 5: organise ideas within and between paragraphs

Make sure that when you write:

- your ideas are linked within paragraphs
- each paragraph is linked to the one it follows
- you use quotation marks.

Step 6: write your conclusion

Re-read the question. Restate two or three key points you want to emphasise. You could add a comment on how successful you think the writer is in showing us these people.

Step 7: feedback

Re-read what you have written. Copy the checklist below and, for each statement, award yourself ☆ or ☆☆ or ☆☆☆ depending on how well you think you have done:

✓ My introduction lets the reader know what my essay will be about.
✓ I used my notes to help me plan and write my essay.
✓ I have developed my ideas in paragraphs.
✓ My paragraphs follow on from each other in a logical order.
✓ I have written about all the main people in the story.
✓ I have used quotations to support my points.
✓ I have summarised my key points and expressed my opinion in my conclusion.

Where you have awarded yourself ☆ or ☆☆, think about how you could improve your answer.

Progress check

1 Look back at the stories you have read in this unit. Place them in order of preference and give **three** reasons for your first choice.

2 Since your last progress check you have:
- worked in a group to compare two stories
- made notes in response to questions on a short story
- used role play to explore issues
- written about an aspect of a short story.

Place these points in order (1–4, starting with the one you think you did best).

3 For each one, write a short report (two to five sentences) on what you achieved and ways in which you could improve.

Assessment task

Understanding culture

You are going to read a short story called 'A Morning Swim' and answer the six questions below. You will be assessed on the way you:

- ✓ show understanding of the culture in which the story is set
- ✓ show awareness of the writer's point of view
- ✓ develop appropriate opinions and judgements on the text
- ✓ use evidence from the text to support the points you make.

First read the story on page 116 closely.

1 List all the details that tell you things about the culture in which this story is set.

2 Choose **three** details from your list and explain how these are similar to or different from your own culture.

3 How does the writer show that diving in the river is not a pleasant thing to do? Make as many points as you can, and use evidence from the text to support each one.

4 Rashid takes the coins that people throw into the river as religious offerings. Imagine you are Rashid. You have been asked to write about what your life is like and to explain why you do what you do. Use details from the text to help you. Aim to write about 200–250 words.

5 Do you think the writer approves or disapproves of what Rashid does? Give reasons for your answer, based on the text.

6 Do you approve or disapprove of what Rashid does? Give your reasons.

The author, Madhulika Liddle, is from New Delhi, India. She wrote 'A Morning Swim' after reading in a newspaper about a young boy who dives into the Yamuna River to make a living from the coins flung into it by worshippers.

A Morning Swim

The fog hung, forbidding. Over the Yamuna.

The water would be icy today, thought Rashid, as he huddled beside Imam Miyan's rickety tea-stall, chewing a stale rusk. There were few people about at this hour of the morning; just the rickshaw-pullers, and the beggars. It was so cold, there'd probably be
5   nobody at the river either.

Imam Miyan's hefty fist clouted Rashid, half-affectionately.

'Eat up, you swine! Do you want to be late? Better get there before the fog lifts and people start arriving.'

Rashid nodded, his thin shoulder hurting with the blow. Not that he would ever protest;
10 Imam Miyan was the only adult who was even remotely kind to him; and when you were just eight years old and an orphan, kindness mattered a hell of a lot. Rashid summoned up a watery smile, but kept quiet. As far back as he could remember, he had been having breakfast – a crumbly rusk and a cup of tea – at Imam Miyan's stall. Whether his parents had been friends of Imam Miyan's he neither knew nor cared; all that mattered was that
15 Imam Miyan was good – sometimes.

Rashid finished the rusk and dug out a coin to pay, but he was lucky today – Imam Miyan refused the rupee.

Bihari, three years older than Rashid, was waiting at the corner, his scabby knees knocking together with the cold. They walked together to the riverside, and Bihari muttered,
20 'Do you want to go in today? It'll be like ice.'

Rashid nodded, trying to push away the thought of the chill water, the itching rash on his body and the stench that awaited him. They had reached the stone steps leading down to the water, and he stripped hurriedly, handing his clothes over to Bihari.

The river was a swirling mass of sewage, carrying with it plastic bags, wilted marigolds
25 and garbage. A sacred river, they called it – sacred enough for the ashes of the dead, from the cremation ground upriver, to be ceremonially immersed in it. Ashes, with bits of charred bone sometimes, wrapped in red cloth, all of it whirling down river, somewhere.

Rashid dived.

It was cold. Cold and opaque, wrapping its foul, grasping fingers about his thin little body,
30 numbing his senses with its rotting presence, encasing him in an envelope of slime. Rashid plunged, deep and swift, down to the riverbed. It was murky and horrible, but he swam around, in widening circles, till his lungs felt as if they would burst, and then he rose, gasping, to the surface.

A few gulps of cold air, and then he was diving down again, into the depths of the
35 Yamuna. Six dives it took before he hauled himself out, shivering and retching. Bihari was sitting on his haunches, sifting hurriedly through a pile of slime, but he rose to help Rashid up the steps, dripping and exhausted. Rashid shrugged on his ragged clothes, watching Bihari through a putrid, shivering daze. After a moment, he said,

'Come along. People have started coming; it wouldn't do to get caught.'
40 Bihari stood up, and with their sodden, stinking burden, the two boys began walking back to the slums, Rashid still wet. He glanced back once over his shoulder, and saw men, wrapped in white, already beginning to go down the steps to the river. Chanting, breathing prayers, bringing with them flowers and fruit, incense and coins – all to be thrown into this sacred, smelly river. New coins, bright and shining – offerings to the Yamuna – and Rashid's
45 daily earnings.

5 Target audience

The bigger picture

In this unit you will explore how writers of non-fiction develop ideas, sometimes in amusing ways. You will consider how arguments are constructed and how points can be presented persuasively. At the end of the unit you will write your own counter-argument.

WHAT? You will:
- examine how writers target purpose and audience
- identify features of informal and formal writing
- use these features in your own writing
- examine how an argument is structured

HOW? by:
- analysing a range of non-fiction texts
- learning more about the passive voice, sentence structures, connectives and rhetorical devices
- applying what you have learnt in different writing tasks
- analysing aspects of an argument to work out how it challenges a commonly held viewpoint

WHY? because:
- writers have more effect when they closely target purpose and audience
- many areas of work and life require you to write in a formal way
- points are made most effectively when appropriate devices are used
- the ability to structure an argument, both in speech and writing, helps you to achieve the things you want.

Purpose and audience

When something is written it has:

- an intended **purpose** – the reason or reasons for which it is written
- an intended **audience** – the reader or readers for whom it is written.

We can work out the intended purpose and audience of a piece of writing by looking for clues in the text. Answer the questions on Text A to help you work out its purpose and audience.

Text A

What type of text is this? How do you know?

What is it about?

What is the writer trying to do?

Who is the intended reader? Why do you think this?

Seaside hotel in guide for bikers

The Donnington Hotel in Scarborough is one of hundreds of pubs, bars and hotels to appear in the 2005 edition of Britain's Ultimate Guide to Biker-friendly Stop-offs.

The guide's authors say it aims to tackle prejudices against bikers who sometimes find businesses refuse to serve people wearing leathers and carrying helmets.

Jane Hunt, of the guide, said: 'Touring the country is a passion for motorcyclists, which is why catering establishments should make themselves known as being biker-friendly.'

Activity 1

1 Read Texts B to D. Copy and complete the table below.
The first row has been filled in to help you get started.

Text	What is it? How do you know this?	What is its intended purpose?	Who is it written for?
A	Newspaper article – headline – set in columns	Trying to interest and inform	Readers of the newspaper – probably local people – probably adults
B			

2 Check your answers with a partner's. Talk about any differences and amend your answers if you need to.

Text B

Sunday, 5 April 1992

I'm trying to concentrate so I can do my homework (reading), but I simply can't. Something is going on in town. You can hear gunfire from the hills. Columns of people are spreading out from Dobrinja. They're trying to stop something, but they themselves don't know what. You can simply feel that something is coming, something very bad. On TV I see people in front of the B-H parliament building. The radio keeps playing the same song: 'Sarajevo, My Love'. That's all very nice, but my stomach is still in knots and I can't concentrate on my homework any more. Mimmy, I'm afraid of WAR!!!

Zlata

Text C

Using your VS2002
Making and ending calls

Lift the handset off the base or charger and press the **Talk** button. The display shows the
(EXT symbol and the green In-use light on the base comes on.

> The display on the other handsets will show the EXT symbol while the line is in use.

When you hear the dial tone, dial the number you require. The number appears in the display and is dialled. After a short delay the call timer will start timing the call.

Text D

Motorcycle emptiness
Torque is cheap with two commentaries

From the Producer of *The Fast And The Furious*, *xXx* and *S.W.A.T.* comes another larger-than-life no-brainer – *Torque*. Ice Cube (*Barbershop*), Martin Henderson (*The Ring*), Monet Mazur (*40 Days, 40 Nights*) and Jay Hernandez (*Crazy/Beautiful*) try to shout above the roar of motorbike engines from 18 May.

When Biker Cary Ford (Henderson) returns to LA after stealing motorcycles belonging to a ruthless drug dealer and biker gang leader, he discovers he's been framed for the murder of Junior, younger brother of Trey (Cube), fearsome leader of the Reapers motorcycle gang. Ford must contend with a vengeful Trey, the equally fearsome girlfriend (Mazur) he left behind and an FBI agent hot on his trail.

Director Joseph Kahn makes the inevitable leap to motion pictures after a music video career that has seen him work with U2, Moby, Britney Spears, Aerosmith, Destiny's Child and Eminem. Kahn joins his cast for one commentary then the creative team record a second. A featurette charts the racing and train-chase sequences from animatic rendering through to the final edit.

Elsewhere, Warner Home Video provides the 'Lean Low' video by Youngbloodz. There's an Easter egg too. Price is $27.95.

Informal writing

It is important that when you write or speak you know your purpose and audience. This knowledge will influence:

- what you write or say
- how you write or say it.

You need to vary the formality of your speech and writing to suit your audience and purpose. If you get the level of formality wrong, your speech or writing will be less effective.

The text below is taken from a book written by two doctors. They wanted to write about teenage health problems in a way that would interest teenagers. To do this, they created Pete Payne and wrote his diary, *The Diary of a Teenage Health Freak*. The diary starts with a profile of the main character. Read it closely before completing Activities 2 and 3.

About this Diary's Writer

GENERAL INFORMATION

My name Peter H. (daren't tell you the rest) Payne.

Nickname 'Know-all Pete'.

Date of birth 17th December

Age 14 years and 1 month – year 9 at school.

Born according to my Mum, half-way down the corridor at the hospital on the way to the labour room.

Address 18 Clifton Road, Hawsley, London.

Hobbies picking my nose, watching telly, computer games, worrying about myself, teasing my younger sister and hacking into her e-mails, annoying people by being a know-all, collecting medical facts, reading FHM, having accidents, my body – tackle and all.

Heroes David Beckham, Nelson Mandela, myself, Sam's dad, whoever it was discovered penicillin but I can't remember who it was, Lara Croft, Harry Potter, Buffy.

What I'll be when I grow up myself, a famous scientist, very rich, and very, very attractive to girls.

Personality at the moment shy, awkward, unattractive to girls, afraid of life, shirker at washing up, tease (especially of my sister Susie), bad at sport, bit of a nerd (doing homework before watching telly), trying to be cool.

Worries catching AIDS, GCSEs, growing up and having a really boring job.

PHYSICAL MAKE-UP

Sex male and becoming more so.

Height 5 feet 4 inches against my door.

Weight 58 kilos but ate a big dinner.

Hair colour brown.

Eye colour brown to match.

Distinguishing marks the whole of me but especially the brown birth-mark on my bum, which I want to show to my girlfriend Cills.

Activity 2

1 Below is a list of features that help to make this text informal. Look back through the text and list as many examples of each feature as you can.
- omission: two words are merged into one by replacing a letter or letters with an apostrophe
- addressing the reader directly
- using slang (non-standard English)
- using partial or incomplete sentences
- written in the first person.

2 Make a note of any other features that you think help to create informality.

Activity 3

1 Write a profile of yourself or a member of your family. Use some, or all, of the features listed in Activity 2 that helped to make the writing informal. You can make your profile funny if you want to.

2 When you have completed your profile:
- highlight and label the features you have used to make it informal
- check these against the features listed in Activity 2
- if you have used less than three features, add more.

From informal to formal writing

You have seen how a writer can adapt language to create an informal tone. There are different levels of informality and formality. You need to be aware of these, both as a reader and a writer.

Texts A–D on page 122 are all to do with the same event: a wedding. However, they differ in:
- their intended purposes and audience
- the level of formality they use.

Activity 4

1 Read Texts A–D. For each one, identify:
- the intended purpose
- the intended audience.

2 Using what you already know about informal and formal writing, place the four texts in order of formality with the most formal first.

3 What features of each text helped you to decide whether it was more or less formal than the other texts?

You could record your answers in a table like the one below.

Text	Intended purpose	Intended audience	Order of formality	Features of formality/informality
A				1 2
B				1 2

Text A

The wedding of Rachel Matthews and Paul Jones took place at Bracken Parish Church at 3pm on Saturday, 31st December. A beautiful cream silk organza dress, beaded with pearls, was worn by the bride. She was attended by three bridesmaids, wearing chocolate silk dresses. Silk roses were used to adorn the church pews and the altar. The groom, who is the son of Mr and Mrs H. Jones, was accompanied by his brother, Michael, as best man. The bride was given away by her father, Mr D. Matthews …

Text B

Hey beth, the date is fixd 4 th weding, ur invo shud b on its way, im so excitd i cnt wait hpe u'l both b able 2 cum.
Loadsa luv rach xxx

Text C

Delete Reply Reply All Forward Print

Julia says:
It was a really good evening. All the old crowd from school were there.
Aaahh … Rach looked fabulous! She wore a lovely silk dress with lots of pearly beads all over it. She looked really happy.

Louise says:
What's Paul like?

Oh … he seemed good … yeah. I wasn't talking to him for long but he really made us laugh. He was telling us about how the best man couldn't find the ring.

 Send»

Text D

You don't need a ticket or an advance reservation. Just make your way to our wedding celebration.

Rachel and Paul will be married on Saturday, 31st December 2005 at Bracken Parish Church.

Please join us for our evening celebration
at Trident Lock Golf Centre
from 7pm onwards.

Please reply to
19 Trent Avenue, Bracken, Derbyshire DE2 9PT

The active and passive voices

A feature of some formal writing is the use of the passive voice. Many verbs can be active or passive.

When the verb is active, the subject performs the action, for example:

The bride wore a lovely silk dress with lots of pearly beads all over it.
 ↓   ↓
subject verb

This is called the **active voice**; it is more direct and personal.

When the verb is passive, the subject is on the receiving end of the action, for example:

A beautiful cream silk organza dress, beaded with pearls, was worn by the bride.
          ↓   ↓
        subject   verb

This is called the **passive voice**; it creates a more distant and impersonal tone.

Activity 5

1 Sort the following sentences into active and passive.
- You are invited to attend.
- Dinner will be provided.
- You should wear formal dress.
- Music will be played by a band.
- The bar will be closed at midnight.
- Mr Jones invites you to attend.
- The hotel will provide dinner.
- Formal dress should be worn.
- A band will play music.
- The bar will close at midnight.

2 Your school is holding a Leavers' Ball for its oldest students.
   a Design and write the Head Teacher's invitation to the students. Use a formal tone and make some use of the passive voice. You could borrow some phrases from Question 1.
   b Write an e-mail from one student to another about the Ball. Include some features of informal writing. You could remind yourself of these by re-reading Activity 2.

3 Annotate your writing to show which features are formal and which are informal.

Examining a formal report

When writing formal English you should always use standard English. You should avoid using slang or omission. Writers of formal English tend to use a wide range of words. Because they are often writing for an adult audience, they use an adult vocabulary range.

Activity 6

1 Read the text on page 125 closely. It is taken from a report on modern families, written for parents and other adults interested in family life. As you are reading:
   - write down any words unfamiliar to you
   - make a note of what you think these words might mean, based on your understanding of their context (what comes before and after them).

2 When you have finished reading:
   - look up the words in a dictionary
   - make a note of the meaning you think is the correct one
   - suggest simpler, more familiar words that could have been used. Why do you think the writer chose the more complex words?

3 To check your understanding of the text, work with a partner. Take it in turns to explain what each paragraph is about. You could start by saying: 'This paragraph explains that/informs us that/suggests that …'

Sharpen spelling

Spelling the -*shun* words

The -*shun* ending to words can be spelt in different ways.

-*tion* is the most common, as in:

transition   addition   consumption

-*cian* is used for words that have a root ending in -c, for example:

magician   technician   dietician

-*sion* is used for words that end in -s or -d, for example:

possess → possession   extend → extension

-*sian* is used for many nationalities, for example:

Asian   Persian   Russian

Put the correct -*shun* ending onto the following words:

electri_____   impres_____   combina_____

politi_____   restora_____   Polyne_____

descrip_____   explo_____   permis_____

confu_____   mathemati_____   Malay_____

The Testing Teens

Three-quarters of parents think that the teenage years are difficult. Half of all parents (51 per cent) surveyed stated that thirteen to fifteen years were the most difficult ages to deal with, whilst almost a quarter of them (24 per cent) stated that sixteen to eighteen years were the most difficult.

The challenges of the difficult transition to the teenage years are well-documented. This is a time of considerable biological changes. It is also when young people are seeking and demanding greater independence. They have to make the transition to secondary school where exams loom and peer pressure can increase. Parents, as well as teenagers, have to find ways to negotiate these changes.

'Between thirteen and fifteen she was most uneasy about who she was, what kind of friends she wanted to have and so on. Making her feel confident about that and helping her was difficult. It got to a stage where we sat down together to talk about things like what time to go out with friends, how late she could stay out, what was safe, etc.'

'At thirteen they think that they know it all and want to try everything out. My job as a parent is to try to guide them through what's right and wrong.'

The emphasis on the early teens as the most difficult time suggests that the ages from thirteen to fifteen represent a crucial stage in children's development. Parents may have thirteen years of experience under their belt but the transition to the teen years may make them feel like they are starting from scratch.

Statistics support parents in their view that the ages from thirteen to fifteen are challenging. They show significant changes in young people's attitudes, behaviour and exposure to outside influences during this time. In addition to the potentially difficult move to secondary school, it is clear that the early teens are a time for experimentation and testing boundaries. One national survey of secondary school students demonstrates that young people's reports of involvement in problem behaviour such as vandalising property and shoplifting peak at the ages of fourteen and fifteen. It is, however, still only a minority that get involved. The same survey shows that young people's reported consumption of alcohol rises sharply during these years. While less than 10 per cent of eleven- and twelve-year-olds report drinking regularly, 30 per cent of fourteen- and fifteen-year-olds do so.

Many parents accept this difficult transition as a normal part of growing up. For the majority, while the teen years can be difficult, they are still relatively trouble-free years. For most it is a challenging time rather than a time of crisis.

from The Lever Fabargé Family Report 2004

125

Sentence structures

Formal writing usually contains a wider range of sentence structures than informal writing. There are three main types of sentences: a simple sentence, a compound sentence and a complex sentence.

A simple sentence contains one main clause. A main clause is a group of words that usually contains a subject and a verb and that makes sense on its own:

This is a time of considerable biological changes.

is

subject

A compound sentence has two or more main clauses joined by a connective. The common connectives are used to link the clauses of a compound sentence: *and, or,* and *but, so.*

They have to make the transition to secondary school where exams loom and peer pressure can increase.

connective

A complex sentence consists of a main clause (which makes complete sense on its own) and one or more subordinate clauses. A subordinate clause is part of the main clause and cannot stand alone; it is usually separated from the main clause by a comma.

subordinate clause   comma

In addition to the potentially difficult transition to secondary school, it is clear that the early teens are a time for experimentation and testing boundaries.

main clause

Activity 7

You can make your writing more interesting by using a range of sentence structures. Here is an example:

a Young people often say they have no money. (simple)
b Young people usually say they have no money but adults often think they have too much. (compound)
c Although young people usually say they have no money, research shows they are spending increasing amounts on CDs and clothes. (complex)

From each of the following simple sentences, develop one compound and one complex sentence:

- Some old people feel threatened by young people.
- Students are quick to grasp new technologies.
- Saturday jobs provide useful work experience.

Balancing information

Some connectives tend to be used more in formal writing than in informal writing. The connectives *while* and *whilst* have similar meanings, and are used several times in the text on page 125. They are used to balance two pieces of information, for example:

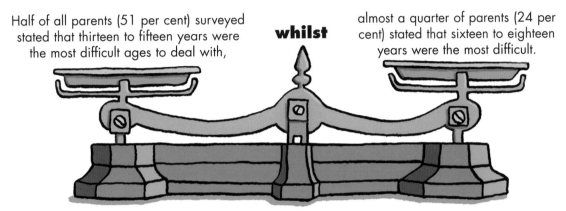

Half of all parents (51 per cent) surveyed stated that thirteen to fifteen years were the most difficult ages to deal with,

whilst

almost a quarter of parents (24 per cent) stated that sixteen to eighteen years were the most difficult.

Activity 8

1 Separate the different pieces of information that are balanced in the sentences below.

  a While less than 10 per cent of eleven and twelve year-olds report drinking regularly, 30 per cent of fourteen and fifteen year-olds do so.

  b For the majority, while the teen years can be difficult, they are still relatively trouble-free years.

2 The six sentences below have been split in two and placed in two columns. Read the two sets of halves, think about how the ideas are balanced, and match the correct number to its corresponding letter.

1 On school exclusions, while 7 per cent of ten- and eleven-year-olds have been excluded from school,

2 Mothers are more involved in care-giving,

3 While it is normal for parents to discuss teething problems or the 'terrible twos',

4 Around 10 per cent of mothers and fathers state that more support from friends and family would most improve their life as a parent,

5 While the teenage years can be a difficult time for most parents,

6 Forty-six per cent of parents were 'very satisfied' with their life as a parent,

A we leave parents to cope with 'testing teens' largely in silence.

B they are genuinely challenging for a minority who really struggle.

C whilst 48 per cent stated that they were 'quite satisfied'.

D while another 10 per cent state that being able to meet and talk to other parents of teenagers would help them out most.

E this figure has more than doubled by the ages of fourteen and fifteen.

F while fathers' contact tends to be focused on joint leisure activities.

Paragraphs

Writers use paragraphs to help organise ideas so that readers can follow them. Each paragraph should introduce a new idea but be closely connected with what went before. A reader should be able to identify the key point explored in each paragraph.

Activity 9

1 Re-read the following paragraphs from the 'Testing Teens' text. Read the notes and answer the questions to help you understand how the paragraphs are structured and linked.

A **key point** is made in the first sentence.

a What does the second sentence do?

Pronouns are used to link ideas and avoid repetition.

b What pronoun replaces the word *parents* in line 5?

c What pronoun is used in place of 'young people' in the second paragraph?

Three-quarters of parents think that the teenage years are difficult. Half of all parents (51 per cent) surveyed stated that thirteen to fifteen years were the most difficult ages to deal with, whilst almost a
5 quarter of them (24 per cent) stated that sixteen to eighteen years were the most difficult.

The challenges of the difficult transition to the teenage years are well documented. This is a time of considerable biological changes. It is also one when
10 young people are seeking and demanding greater independence. They have to make the transition to secondary school where exams loom and peer pressure can increase. Parents, as well as teenagers, have to find ways to negotiate these changes.

Paragraphs are often **linked by ideas**.

d Find and write down the words that link the second paragraph to the first.

The **focus** of the first paragraph is on parents.

e Who does the second paragraph focus on?

f How does the final sentence bring the two together?

Think about **the way the report is written**.

g When is the present tense used? When is the past tense used?
h Is the report written in the first or the third person?

2 Write two or three paragraphs of a formal report, showing why Year 9 can be difficult for some young people. The pictures on the next page might give you some ideas. Make sure you:
- write in the present tense
- write in the third person
- start each paragraph with a key point and develop it in the paragraph
- have a clear link in ideas between the first and the second paragraph
- use pronouns where appropriate
- use a range of simple, compound and complex sentences.

Leave space on either side of your writing for annotations.

Feedback

1 Swap your paragraphs with a partner. Find and annotate the features of formal writing bulleted in Activity 9, question 2.
2 When your work is returned to you, check you have all the features annotated. If you have missed anything, think about how you could have included it in your writing and make notes on what you could have done.

Progress check

In this unit you have studied features of informal and formal writing.
1 Identify **three** differences between informal and formal English.
2 When might you use formal English?
3 What is the difference between the active and the passive voice?
4 What is a compound sentence? Write an example of one.
5 What is a complex sentence? Write an example of one.
6 Read the following pairs of words and phrases. For each pair, choose the one that is the more formal:

a	makes it sound as if	suggests that	**e** challenging	not easy
b	changeover	transition	**f** demonstrates	shows
c	documented	written down	**g** small number	minority
d	work out	negotiate		

If you are unsure about any of the answers, check back through the unit before moving on.

Writing to amuse

Humour can be found in informal and formal writing. You are going to look at how humour is created in two non-fiction texts. The first is written in informal English and the second in formal English.

The text on the opposite page is taken from a later section of *The Diary of a Teenage Health Freak*. Remember that the doctors who wrote this wanted to communicate health information to teenagers in a lively and amusing way. In this passage, Peter is visiting the dentist.

Highlight thinking

Critical thinking: peer evaluation

Peer evaluation means working with someone who is doing the same sort of work as you are, to help you both improve. It is a useful way of thinking through your work because:

- two heads are better than one – a partner can identify areas for development that you might miss
- talking through problems and issues in your work with someone else helps you to understand them more clearly yourself.

Activity 10

1 Read the text and list the information you are given about dental care. Questions 2–4 will help you to focus on how humour is created in the text.

2 Here is a list of some of the techniques the writers use to create humour:

alliteration   **rhyme**   **comparison**   **imitation**   **exaggeration**

Which technique(s) do the writers use to:
- suggest that there are not many National Health Service dentists
- bring humour into Peter's description of his old dentist
- make the description of the lips funny
- describe the unpleasantness of a filling
- bring humour to the end of Tuesday's entry?

3 Explain how the writer creates humour in the entry for Friday 25th October.

4 Imagine you are the writer of this diary. You want to tell teenagers how to be safe if they are having their body pierced. Write the opening 10–20 lines of a diary entry that presents the following information in an amusing way.
- Choose a well-established body piercer.
- Make sure that the piercing studio is spotless and meets local health authority standards.
- Make sure the piercer:
  - ✓ belongs to the association of professional piercers   ✓ has had first-aid training
  - ✓ uses brand-new needles   ✓ wears disposable gloves.

You do not need to include all the information, but do aim to amuse your reader.

Feedback

1 Ask a partner to read your diary entry. They should:
   - number the points of information you give
   - underline the parts they think are funny
   - make suggestions for how you could make it funnier.

2 When your partner returns your writing, try to include some or all of their suggestions.

Tuesday 23rd October Mum took us to a new dentist. Said we were lucky to find one who still worked for the National Health Service, and would give us our treatment free if we were under eighteen. In some places they're rarer than hen's teeth nowadays … ha, ha.

Susie had this final fitting for her brace, so Mum suddenly had to remember me too, didn't she? Was scared stiff of my old dentist, who would pin me to the chair and be furious if I so much as screamed occasionally. She went bankrupt. Served her right. Don't know why they don't replace dentists with robots, like the ones that build cars.

Dentists are bigger liars than politicians. They say they won't hurt, but you come out in agony, with lips feeling the size of a blue baboon's bum. But some have traces of being human – like this new one. He's nice – has space gadgets and makes jokes all the time. With my mouth full of bits of metal, it's easier to laugh than answer stupid questions. Says it's boring dealing with rotten teeth every day, just cos people can't be bothered to clean them. Gave me a leaflet to read while he was poking around in Susie's mouth.

GOOD TEETH, GOOD LOOKS

Good teeth, bad teeth – it's not down to luck
Remember, neglect your teeth and they soon start to look dingy. Worse still, they can decay and cause pain. And they can also create an unpleasant smell and taste in your mouth. Despite what you may have heard, it's not chance that will help you keep your teeth and your looks. It's knowing what to do and then doing it.

ENEMIES
'Tooth decay'
What happens is that sugar and bacteria in the mouth get together and make an acid. This acid attacks the …

Cor! What kind of patronising git wrote that?
Had to have a filling and the worst bit was when he crammed cotton-wool pads, a sucker thing, and a drill into my mouth all at the same time. Thought I was going to drown in my own spit – what a way to go, worse than chlorinated pee.

Meanwhile dentist burbled on about how your teeth need ONE really good, thorough brush every day, with any toothbrush and (most important) with FLUORIDATED toothpaste. He reckoned that if everybody did this – or if the government fluoridated all drinking water, like they do in Moscow, New York, Birmingham, Dublin and Sydney; and if people gave up eating sweets and other sugary things all the time, and just ate them occasionally, say on Wednesdays and Saturdays – then teeth problems would almost disappear and he could retire. The average English schoolchild eats 118 grams of sugar EVERY day. This sugar is turned into acid by bugs in our mouths and starts eating into the enamel of our teeth within a few seconds – uggghhh!
At least I'm not 'brace faced' like Susie!

Friday 25th October Sssusie sssays that it'sss like having ssseventeen sssets of teeth. Ssshe ssspeaks like thisss all the time.

Humour in more formal writing

You saw in the extracts from *The Diary of a Teenage Health Freak* how the writers create humour in describing a familiar situation – a visit to the dentist. The writer of the newspaper article on page 133 also chooses a familiar topic – babies. As you saw on page 124, writers of formal English tend to use an adult vocabulary range.

Activity 11

1 Read the 'Why I Love Fat Babies' article on page 133 closely and:
- write down any unfamiliar words
- note down what the words might mean.

2 When you have finished reading:
- look up the words in a dictionary
- decide which of the possible meanings is the correct one and make a note of it.

In 'Why I Love Fat Babies', the writer uses humour to help to persuade the reader. The questions below will help you to identify how this is done.

Sharpen punctuation

Using a range of punctuation
Knowing how to use a range of punctuation enables you to introduce variety and meaning to your writing.

1 Read the following sentences and list the different punctuation marks used in them.
Infancy is, after all, the last bastion of loveable largeness, the only time – save TV pop contests – when fatness is still truly celebrated. Although adults are prone to poke fun at said infants ('Hey Fatso!' and 'What a porker!' being acceptable for those under fifteen months), big is unquestionably beautiful in baby terms.

2 What do the following punctuation marks allow the writer to do?
- hyphens • brackets • quotation marks

3 Write two sentences about 'Beautiful Babies', in which you experiment with a range of punctuation.

Activity 12

1 How many questions are asked in lines 1–11? How do these help to build a connection between the writer and the reader?

2 The writer lists adjectives to create humour and a picture for the reader, for example: *A <u>big</u>, <u>bouncy</u> dough-ball of an infant, with a <u>cute</u>, <u>carefree</u> smile and an abundance of <u>buoyant</u> ripples.* Find and write down at least **two** other examples of adjectives being used to create humour and a picture for the reader.

3 Find and list **three** examples of the writer comparing a fat baby to food. What impressions of the baby do these create?

4 Alliteration is used to help make this picture of the baby more memorable and to add a touch of fun, for example: *big bouncy; cute carefree*. Find and write down **two** other examples of alliteration.

5 The writer refers to everyday things in the reader's world, for example: *Tesco tiger prawns, TV pop contests.* Find at least **three** other references to everyday things and suggest why the writer includes these.

Why I Love Fat Babies

1 How does the opening immediately make the reader focus on the subject of the article?

Is there anything more pleasing in this life than a fat baby? A big, bouncy dough-ball of an infant, with a cute, carefree smile and an abundance of buoyant ripples? A fat baby is a joy to behold, a blessing to all who see it – and then point and laugh.

2 What types of food is the baby compared to in this paragraph?

My favourite bits? The squidgy face that looks like an unbaked bun. The fingers that resemble Tesco tiger prawns. And those little puckers of flesh around the arms and knees that remind me of pleats on a **Ginster's pasty**. 'Couldn't you just eat it?' someone always declares when holding a fat baby. I breathlessly agree (though drawing the line at discussing serving suggestions).

3 How does the closing sentence make fun of the last question?

4 What word directly links this paragraph with the previous one?

And in our present body-crazed, diet-obsessed state, my love of the fat baby takes on a wider, almost political significance. Infancy is, after all, the last bastion of loveable largeness, the only time – save TV pop contests – when fatness is still truly celebrated. Although adults are prone to poke fun at said infants ('Hey Fatso!' and 'What a porker!' being acceptable for those under fifteen months), big is unquestionably beautiful in baby terms. And unless a relative suggests calling the Guinness Book of Records people, this portliness is merely a sign of ruddy good health. Indeed, research shows that fat babies are less likely to suffer from depression in later years than skinnier ones.

5 How does the closing sentence reinforce the writer's opinion that a fat baby is a healthy one?

Looking like an over-inflated **Cabbage Patch Kid**, this infant exists in a state of pure, bloated innocence. It is blissfully unaware of the social troubles that such fleshiness will bring later on, and mercifully so. Of Atkins diets, leaky **liposuction**, and, at worst, a place on *Celebrity Fit Club*. So make the most of it, baby. Fatness will not always be your friend.

6 How does this comparison sum up the picture of the fat baby that is built in the first two paragraphs?

7 What does the writer do in the last two sentences to change the focus and give the article a clear ending?

Word bank

Ginster's pasty a traditional Cornish pasty that has a crimp along the side
Cabbage Patch Kid a type of doll
liposuction a medical process by which fat is removed

Paragraphs revisited

On page 128 you examined:

- how a key idea was introduced and developed in a paragraph
- how ideas were linked between two paragraphs.

Now you are going to think more about these and about how writers open and close paragraphs.

Activity 13

1 Look back at the article 'Why I Love Fat Babies'. Answer questions 1 to 7 surrounding the article, to help you understand the links within and between paragraphs.

2 Re-read the following paragraph from the article. The writer has used a number of connectives to link the ideas. (Look back to pages 126 and 127 to remind yourself about connectives.) The first two are highlighted for you. Identify and write down the other three connectives in this paragraph. Check your answers with a partner.

> And in our present body-crazed, diet-obsessed state, my love of the fat baby takes on a wider, almost political significance. Infancy is, after all, the last bastion of loveable largeness, the only time – save TV pop contests – when fatness is still truly celebrated. Although adults are prone to poke fun at said infants ('Hey Fatso!' and 'What a porker!' being acceptable for those under fifteen months), big is unquestionably beautiful in baby terms. And unless a relative suggests calling the Guinness Book of Records people, this portliness is merely a sign of ruddy good health. Indeed, research shows that fat babies are less likely to suffer from depression in later years than skinnier ones.

Activity 14

You are going to write a newspaper article entitled **Why I Love** _____.
Your aim is to use humour to persuade others to share your point of view.
Follow Steps 1–5 below.

Step 1

Choose a subject. This could be almost anything, large or small. Here are some suggestions:

Step 2

List five or six reasons that explain your love. Place them in order and delete the weakest.

Step 3

Think of, and write down:
- a good opening question
- a list of adjectives you could use to create humour
- funny comparisons you could make
- alliterations you could use to add fun
- how you could make your subject relevant to your reader.

Step 4

Use your planning to help you write three paragraphs. You should aim to:
- develop your ideas clearly
- sometimes use connectives to link ideas
- make your writing funny
- make clear links between the closing sentence of one paragraph and the opening sentence of the next one.

Step 5

In a group of three or four, compare your articles. Together, decide what comments should be written at the end of each article. These should focus on:
- how clearly the ideas are developed and connected
- how funny the article is
- the links made between and within the paragraphs.

Writers' devices

Writers and speakers use a range of devices to make their words more effective; you will have come across many of these before and in this unit. You need to be able to identify these and work out how they are used by writers.

 Activity 15

On the next page you will find:
- ten examples of different texts (A–J)
- the names of ten linguistic devices (1–10)
- descriptions of each of the ten linguistic devices (I–X)

Read each text carefully. Decide which linguistic device is used in it. Match the linguistic device to the correct description. Record your findings on a table like this. The first one has been done for you.

Text	A	B	C	D	E	F	G	H	I	J
Device	8									
Description	II									

A While awaiting the President's decision, the whole nation holds its breath.

B The people flocked to see it.

C Sometimes we have to be cruel to be kind.

D I came. I saw. I conquered.

E The car drew to a halt. Too late.

F This helpless, defenceless kitten was placed in a box and left to die.

G Freddie Fires First Fusilier

H They fought like two tigers defending their territory.

I Two World Wars and millions dead. Have we learned nothing?

J She was the first through the tape, the first to achieve that time and the first to win gold for her country.

1 Rhetorical question

2 Alliteration

3 Repetition

4 Metaphor

5 Simile

6 Group of three

7 Emotive use of language

8 Hyperbole

9 Contrast

10 Short sentence

I This device helps you to picture something more clearly.

II This device uses exaggeration for effect.

III This device helps to draw readers in and make them think.

IV This device makes a particular phrase more memorable.

V This device groups three ideas together for extra impact.

VI This device uses two opposites to make a point.

VII This device can make you think of something in a completely different way.

VIII This device makes a powerful point with few words.

IX This device gives a particular point extra emphasis.

X This device aims to make the reader feel a particular emotion.

 Feedback

1 Compare your completed table with a partner's.
2 Talk about any differences you may have and the reasons for them.
3 Are there any descriptions that could be used for more than one device?
4 Agree a final order for your table before moving on.

Activity 16

1 The writer of the speech 'Don't Be Scared of Those Sharks', (pages 138–140), uses a number of different devices to help get his points across. Read the text closely and make a list of the devices you find, and their purpose, for example:

List of devices

Line number(s)	Device	Purpose
1 to 3	questions	to make the reader think

Use the list on page 136 to remind you of the devices to look out for. You will not find examples of all of these.

2 Check your list with a partner's. Add to your list any devices that you missed.

Supporting points with evidence

When writing about a text, you often need to refer to particular details in it. You do this mainly to give evidence to support the points you are making.

- Sometimes you will refer to a detail, for example:
  To get the audience to think about the popular image of sharks, the writer mentions the film 'Jaws'.

- Sometimes you will quote directly from the text as evidence. You might want to quote single words or phrases, for example:
  The writer uses a group of three, to emphasise the lack of danger from sharks, when he says they are 'small', 'harmless' and that they don't 'live anywhere near' humans.

Notice how quotation marks are placed around the words that are taken from the text.

- Occasionally, you might want to quote a whole sentence or more as evidence, for example:
  The writer deliberately places a short sentence after a longer one to give extra emphasis to the point being made:
  'Anyone with a pet knows that any animal can become fierce when strangers invade its space. Sharks are just the same.'

Notice how a colon is used to show that the quotation is to follow. The quotation is placed on a new line.

Activity 17

Using what you learnt about the use of devices in Activities 15 and 16, write a paragraph describing the writer's use of devices in 'Don't Be Scared of Those Sharks'. Refer to details in the extract and use quotations as evidence for the things you say.

Don't Be Scared of Those Sharks

What happens to you when you hear the music from the movie *JAWS*?
Do chills run down your spine?
Do you think of sharks coming out of the depths at you?
Our active imaginations have made sharks into modern-day monsters.
5 But do you really know what your chances are of getting attacked by a shark?

Just what is fact?
And what is fantasy?

Well here's the fantasy.
We all know this about sharks, don't we?
10 They're vicious,
they'll eat anything,
they all want to eat people,
and they're everywhere.

Well, just think about this.
15 Most shark species (about 80 per cent) have never even attacked a human.
And of the ones that do, it adds up to about 100 people,
each year,
worldwide …
and most of these victims survive.
20 In fact, most sharks are small, harmless and don't live anywhere near us.

So now that we know the facts, let's look a little more closely at the life of a
shark and how they really behave.
First things first: how keen are they to get themselves some human flesh?
Hardly at all, as it turns out.

25 Their job is to live by eating, breathing and reproducing – just like any other animal.

They eat fish and other marine animals.

People are not part of their normal diet.

And think about this:

30 If white sharks really were attacking humans for food,
why is it that nearly 75 per cent of these attacks are non-fatal?

Why do they stop eating?

The answer, according to most experts, is that they're looking for something with more fat.

35 People are too scrawny.

So why exactly do they attack, if they don't want us?

About the only time sharks attack humans on purpose is when their territory is invaded or their courtship rituals are interrupted.

Anyone with a pet knows that any animal can become fierce when strangers
40 invade its space.

Sharks are just the same.

Most other shark attacks are probably just cases of mistaken identity:
a swimmer's flapping feet and hands may look like the movements of a fish darting through the water;
45 a human, especially one wearing a black wet suit and flippers, may look something like a seal.

But don't even assume that because you can aggravate them, that there's danger waiting on your beach.

The beaches aren't full of great white sharks, just waiting for us.

50 Far from it.

In fact, great whites are relatively uncommon, and they prefer cooler waters.

What's more, in some parts of their range, great whites are close to being endangered.

Jaws got it wrong – it is safe to go into the water.

55 But just for argument's sake even though the odds of you running into one are really remote, let's assume the worst: you've got in the way of a shark.

What will happen to you?

Well, more than likely, you'll come through it okay.

During the majority of attacks, the shark bites the person only once and then 60 retreats.

Ken Goldman, a shark researcher from the Virginia Institute of Marine Science, in Gloucester Point, has been studying great whites in the Farallons for the past seven years.

He says their attacks are very controlled, and so is their feeding behaviour, and 65 that means the idea of a feeding frenzy is just wrong.

So now you know how low the risk is, what can you do to make that risk virtually disappear?

Here's what Canada's Pacific National Aquarium, in Stanley Park have to advise.

– The best prevention for shark attack is common sense.

70 – Avoid swimming between sandbars, near steep drop-offs, near channels or at river mouths where sharks are found.

– Avoid wearing shiny jewelry that might look like the scales of a prey fish, and also bright-colored clothing.

– Avoid spreading blood or human wastes in the water.

75 – If fish start to behave oddly or group in large numbers, leave the area.

– And if, despite all the odds against it happening, you see a shark, the answer is simple:

just leave the water calmly and quickly.

The plain fact is that sharks are not after us.

80 They'd rather eat fish.

Most of them never even come near us, and the ones that do are most likely to do so by mistake, or because we're just in the wrong place.

So the answer is simple:

You have to learn a little about sharks' natural behavior,

85 and that's what you've just done.

You know how unlikely anything bad is to happen,

and you also know how to deal with it if the unlikely actually comes to pass.

And that means you can enjoy yourself in the water.

So rest easy next time you hit the beach

90 – Jaws isn't looking for you.

He's got other fish to fry.

British/American English

There are many spelling differences between British and American English, for example:

British English   American English

jewellery jewelry   coloured colored   behaviour behavior

American English spelling is becoming increasingly familiar through the media, in particular the Internet. Some people, however, object to its use. When writing formally it is best to use the British English spelling.

Write the British English forms of the following:

airplane	cigaret	snowplow	canceled	traveler	center
dialog	pajamas	sulfur	licorice	leukemia	drafty

Making a counter-argument

In 'Don't Be Scared of Those Sharks' the writer challenges the widely held view that sharks are dangerous creatures just waiting for the opportunity to attack people. The writer calls this view the 'fantasy'. From line 14 onwards he starts to develop his counter-argument. His aim is to influence how his audience thinks about sharks. Complete Activity 18 to help you understand how he does this.

Activity 18

1 List the facts the writer uses in lines 14–20.

2 In lines 21–49, he asks some of the questions his audience might want to ask and he answers them, for example:

How keen are they to get themselves some human flesh?

Hardly at all, as it turns out … People are not part of their normal diet.

What other questions does he raise and answer in lines 21–49?

3 Why does the writer refer to *Jaws* in line 54?

4 In lines 55–6 the writer raises the most extreme concern:

But just for argument's, sake, even though the odds of you running into one are really remote, let's assume the worst: you've got in the way of a shark.

How does he then try to put the audience's mind at rest?

5 Why do you think the writer chose to include the advice given in lines 68–78?

6 Towards the end the writer sums up his main points. Where does this summary start? Why do you think he does this?

7 How do the final three lines:

- reinforce the writer's message
- connect with the opening
- use humour for effect?

More about connectives

Connectives are words that connect sentences or clauses within sentences. On page 127 you studied the use of *while* and *whilst*. The connective *but* is used several times in 'Don't Be Scared of Those Sharks'. It is also used to weigh up different ideas. Talk about the different ideas contained in each of the following.

- Our active imaginations have made sharks into modern day monsters. But do you really know what your chances are of getting attacked by a shark?
- Sharks are often called unpredictable but this has been more a reflection of our own knowledge rather than the behavior of the sharks themselves.

Notice how *but* is usually used to give emphasis to the writer's point of view.

Activity 19

Here is a range of connectives you might use when writing an argument:

moreover	while	whilst	alternatively	so	also
therefore	however	anyway	although	but	

1 Copy and complete the paragraph below by deciding which connectives are most appropriate to fill in the blanks.

Some people argue that more money should be spent on cleaning the streets _____1_____ this seems to be such a waste. Surely we should all just make an effort not to put so much litter on them in the first place. I hate to see streets covered in chip papers, coke cans and stuff dropped from other people's mouths. _____2_____, just think of what that money could be spent on. _____3_____ it may not be enough to ease the national debt, it could certainly heat up a few old people's homes in winter. _____4_____, it could be used to provide better care for children in hospital. _____5_____ next time you're about to empty your pockets onto the pavement, use your brain first.

2 Compare your choices with a partner's. Talk about any differences and the reasons for these. Decide on the best choices.

✓ Progress check

When writing a counter-argument you have seen how a writer has:
- used a range of rhetorical devices
- made a range of points
- used factual evidence
- asked the questions the audience might ask
- used connectives to link points.

1 Look back at 'Don't Be Scared of Those Sharks' on pages 138–40. Identify how and where the writer has done each of the bulleted points. Make a note of the line numbers.

2 Write one or two sentences describing how confident you feel about using these features in your own writing.

⬭ Assessment task

Can you argue?

You are going to write your own counter-argument.

You will be assessed on the way you:
- present a clear and developed counter-argument
- organise your ideas into paragraphs
- write in formal standard English
- use a range of writing devices to influence the attitude of your reader.

You may use humour to influence your readers, if you want to.

The following are commonly held views. Your task is to choose one of them and present an argument that runs counter to it. Think carefully about your choice, as you need to be able to make enough points against it to develop a convincing argument.

Young people today have no time for anyone but themselves.

We need to experiment on animals to develop new medicines.

Popular music was of a much higher standard 40 years ago than it is now.

You can tell it's a good school if the children all wear uniform.

Reality TV is the best kind of TV there is.

Far too much money and media coverage is given to footballers.

To write your argument, follow the steps described below.

Step 1

Write the point of view you are going to argue against at the top of your page.
Make notes on:

- the different points you could make against this point of view
- the questions or further points that could be made in support of it.

Step 2

Plan your paragraphs.
Aim to write five paragraphs.
In your first paragraph you should state clearly what point of view you are opposing, for example:

You often hear people complaining about young people today. They say they do nothing but hang around on street corners drinking alcohol. Some even say that ...

Paragraphs 2, 3 and 4 should each develop a separate point in support of your view. Remember to:

- support the points you make with evidence
- make a clear link between your paragraphs.

Your last paragraph should sum up the points you have made, though you could introduce a final new point to really make your reader think.

Step 3

You are almost ready to write. Remember to:

- write in formal standard English
- use connectives to link sentences and ideas within sentences
- use a range of devices to interest your reader, for example, rhetorical questions, contrast, metaphor, etc.

Step 4

Write your argument. Remember to:

- re-read your writing after each paragraph
- check your writing against the objectives listed at the top of page 143.

Step 5

Check your writing.
Read through your writing closely and:

- make sure you have made your points clearly and in an interesting way
- correct any spelling and punctuation errors that you spot.

6 Much ado about Shakespeare

The bigger picture

In this unit you will explore the appeal of Shakespeare's plays in his own time and today. You will then focus on one of his plays, *Much Ado About Nothing*, and explore how its plots, characters, themes and language shape its performance.

WHAT? You will:
- discover how Shakespeare wrote for his audience
- look closely at the plots, characters, themes and language of *Much Ado About Nothing*
- perform extracts from the play
- learn to structure your writing about Shakespeare

HOW? by:
- identifying the appeal of different plots
- exploring the relationships between plots, characters and language
- experimenting with interpretation and performance and their effect on an audience
- practising writing about Shakespeare

WHY? because:
- understanding Shakespeare's appeal will increase his appeal to you
- close investigation of the play helps you to understand how Shakespeare crafted his writing
- Shakespeare wrote his plays for performance in the theatre
- writing successfully about Shakespeare allows you to demonstrate your understanding of his work.

Where's William?

Coming soon:
The Merry Wives
of Windsor
A story of love, money
and hilarious consequences
"If you see only one comedy this year,
make it the Merry Wives!"

You may know some facts about William Shakespeare already. You probably know that he wrote plays. You may know that he was born in 1564, during the reign of Queen Elizabeth I, and died in 1616, when James I had become king.

Activity 1

Study the artist's impression on pages 146–7 of the Globe Theatre in Shakespeare's times. Try to find the man himself, William Shakespeare. What else can you find out about Shakespeare's plays and his work from looking closely at the picture? Use the questions that follow to help you.

1 What else did Shakespeare do in the theatre, apart from writing?

2 What types of plays did Shakespeare write?

3 What was it about Shakespeare's plays that made them so popular?

4 What kind of people went to see Shakespeare's plays?

5 What three things can you see that made the theatre in Shakespeare's time different from a modern theatre?

Shakespeare: the all-round entertainer

Just like Shakespeare's audience, modern audiences like to be entertained in lots of different ways.

Exploring different plots

Activity 2

Look at the ideas below and opposite for a new blockbuster film. Working with a partner, read through the different plots, then answer the questions that follow to help you decide which would be the most popular with audiences.

Plot A

A respected black war hero falls in love with a beautiful white woman. Despite her father's racist objections, they marry and live happily … until the war hero's lieutenant plots to destroy him and his marriage. He lies to the hero, telling him his wife is having an affair with his friend. The hero is so angry and jealous he kills his wife.

Plot B

The leader of a world power believes he has the right to invade and take control of a foreign country. Angered by the foreign ruler's arrogance and insults, he leads his army through a difficult and troubled campaign to a triumphant victory. A true story.

Plot C

A rich old man wants to give all he has to his three daughters before he dies. He asks each one how much she loves him. Two of the daughters lie: they say they love him more than anything in the world. The man is flattered. The third daughter tells the truth – she loves him like a father. The man throws her out of the house without a penny. It is only once he has lost everything, that the man realises only one of his daughters truly loves him. But it is too late – she dies in his arms.

Plot D

A boy and a girl love each other – but the girl's father wants her to marry someone else. The girl and the boy decide to run away together. The girl's friend loves the boy her father wants her to marry – but he doesn't love her. The two couples meet with some powerful magic and chaos follows!

1 Do these plots remind you of anything you have already seen – on television, at the cinema, on the news?

2 Decide which genre, or type of story, each of the plots belongs to – action, romance, thriller, drama, comedy or something else?

3 Would these stories appeal to men, women, boys, girls or a combination?

4 Why might these stories appeal to audiences? Match plots A–D with reasons i–v below. Remember that a plot might appeal to an audience for more than one reason.
   i   Makes the audience forget about the real world.
   ii Makes the audience think about the world we live in.
   iii Makes the audience think about their own lives and what is important.
   iv Will appeal to the audience's feelings and emotions.
   v   Other reasons. What are they?

5 a Using your answers to questions 1 to 4, talk to a partner and decide which of these plots would appeal to the widest audience. Put them in order from the most popular to the least popular.
   b Write a paragraph about the plot you decided would be most popular. Explain who it would appeal to – and why.
   c What features could you add to the plot to make it appeal to an even larger audience?

All four of the plots on pages 148–9 have been used in films and in theatres. Plot A is the story of *Othello*. Plot B is the story of *Henry the Fifth*. Plot C is the story of *King Lear*, and Plot D is the story of A *Midsummer Night's Dream*. They are all plays written by Shakespeare.

Shakespeare was and is a great entertainer, giving audiences laughter, tears, suspense, adventure, horror … in fact, all the things that drama and comedy, on television and at the cinema, give audiences in the twenty-first century. Here are three more of his plots.

> **E** A man and a woman bicker and insult each other every time they meet. He says he'll never marry her. She says she can't stand him either.
>
> **F** Two young lovers are torn apart because an evil, lying villain with a grudge makes the man think the woman is unfaithful.
>
> **G** Police chase an evil villain but are so stupid and disorganised they cannot arrest him.

Activity 3

You are going to explore how different genres, or types of story, can be woven together.

1 Write an ending for each of the three plots above. Try to make one a romantic story, one an action adventure and one a comedy.

2 Working with a partner, write a plot summary that combines plots F and G into one story. Then write a plot that combines *all three plots* into one story.

3 Decide which of your plots would be most popular with audiences: choose one from E, F or G, or the combination of two or three mixed together. Write two or three sentences explaining your decision.

Much Ado About Nothing

All three of the stories you have been working on are from Shakespeare's *Much Ado About Nothing*. When modern audiences watch television they can choose from comedies, soaps, drama, news, just by pressing a button on the remote control. In Shakespeare's time, a play had to please as many people as possible, so it had to have a mix of ingredients and, sometimes, two or three different plots going on at the same time – some to make the audience laugh, some to make them cry, and some for excitement and adventure.

Introducing Beatrice and Benedick

You are now going to look in detail at one of the plots from *Much Ado About Nothing*: the story of Benedick and Beatrice, the arguing lovers. Later you will look at the rest of the play. On pages 152–3 is a storyboard of the Beatrice and Benedick story. The characters you will meet are described below.

Don Pedro:
a prince, just back from a victorious war. Benedick fights in his army.

Claudio:
a friend of Benedick. They fought together for Don Pedro.

Leonato:
Beatrice's uncle.

Benedick:
a proud and vain young soldier. Thinks he knows it all and that falling in love is a sign of weakness.

Beatrice:
young and beautiful. Thinks women are just as intelligent as men and should be independent, making their own minds up about whether and who they'll marry.

Hero:
Leonato's daughter. Beatrice's cousin. Tricks Beatrice into believing that Benedick loves her.

Ursula:
Hero's serving woman. Helps Beatrice with her trick.

These three trick Benedick into thinking that Beatrice loves him.

Activity 4

1 Look at the picture above and choose one of the characters.

2 Now, working with a partner, try to find out which character they have chosen by asking questions. Your partner is only allowed to answer 'yes' or 'no'. You only have five questions – so think carefully about what you want to ask.

The Beatrice and Benedick Story

(1) How many hath he killed? For indeed, I promised to eat all of his killing.

Leonato hears that Don Pedro, Claudio and Benedick are on their way back from the war to visit him. Beatrice asks the messenger how well Benedick did in the battle. She mocked him before he went.

(2) There is a kind of merry war betwixt Signor Benedick and her.

Leonato explains that his niece Beatrice is always bickering with Benedick.

(3) It is certain I am loved of all ladies, only you excepted.

I wonder that you will still be talking, Signor Benedick, nobody marks you.

The visitors arrive – and the insults between Benedick and Beatrice begin. Beatrice is surprised that Benedick bothers speaking when no one is taking any notice of him. Benedick points out that he is very popular with women – except for one.

(4) I shall see thee, 'ere I die, look pale with love.

I will live a bachelor.

With anger, with sickness, or with hunger, my lord, not with love.

Benedick is sure he will never marry. Don Pedro is not so sure …

(5) I had rather hear my dog bark at a crow than a man swear he loves me.

Coincidentally, Beatrice tells Benedick exactly the same thing. She does not want to hear that any man loves her.

(6) She were an excellent wife for Benedick … I will undertake to bring Signor Benedick and the Lady Beatrice into a mountain of affection the one with the other.

Don Pedro thinks Beatrice and Benedick are well suited. He asks Leonato, Claudio and Hero to help him bring them together.

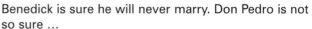

The plot is hatched. Don Pedro, Leonato and Claudio let Benedick overhear that Beatrice loves him.

Benedick believes them. He sees Beatrice approaching and notices her beauty and even thinks he sees love in her eyes …

A little later on, Hero and her servant, Ursula, pull the same trick on Beatrice. They discuss Benedick's love knowing that Beatrice is listening.

Beatrice believes them and decides she will love Benedick back.

Benedick and Beatrice confess their love for each other. But Beatrice demands that he prove it – by taking revenge on Claudio for treating her cousin, Hero, so badly.

Claudio and Hero's problems are all sorted out. They are married – and so are Beatrice and Benedick, still bickering.

Activity 5

You now need to make sure you know the story of Beatrice and Benedick and know all about the characters involved in their story.

1 Working in a group, prepare a short performance of one of the frames from the storyboard on pages 152–3. Choose a narrator to read the modern English caption and actors to perform Shakespeare's lines. Use the questions below to help you prepare.

- How are the characters positioned in relation to one another?
- How will the characters move or stand?
- How will the characters speak?
- How will the characters react to one another?

2 Perform your 'frame' as part of a sequence around the class.

 **Feedback**

Look at this mixed-up list of the events in the Beatrice and Benedick story.

- Beatrice and Benedick are married.
- Hero makes sure Beatrice overhears her saying that Benedick loves her.
- Don Pedro, Leonato and Claudio make sure Benedick overhears them saying that Beatrice loves him.
- Beatrice and Benedick admit their love to each other.
- Beatrice and Benedick love to insult each other.
- Don Pedro, Leonato and Claudio decide to trick Beatrice and Benedick.
- Beatrice and Benedick realise that they do love each other.
- Beatrice and Benedick are sure they will never marry anyone – and certainly not each other.

1 Put the events in the correct order and number them 1–8.

2 Now re-tell the story to a partner without looking at your list of events. Ask your partner to check your story against their list. They should write down the number of each event you tell well, and the number of each event you forget or don't make clear.

3 With your partner, look at the events you forgot and try the task again.

4 Which medal would you award yourself for this task?

I know some of the story.

I know most of the story.

I know all of the story.

Exploring character – Beatrice and Benedick

You are now going to look more closely at what Beatrice and Benedick say and do, what they think and what this tells us about them.

Activity 6

Look again at the storyboard on pages 152–3, concentrating on the characters of Beatrice and Benedick.

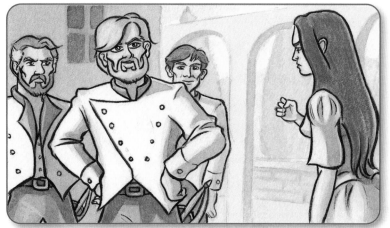

1 Copy and complete the three sentences below to explore the characters' attitudes to themselves and each other.

- Benedick thinks that ...
- Beatrice thinks that ...
- They both think that ...

2 Now, looking at your answers to question 1, complete these three sentences with as many different words as you can to describe their characters.

- Benedick is ...
- Beatrice is ...
- Both of them are ...

3 Choose one word from each of your sentences that you think really sums up these characters. Underline it and choose a quotation from the characters on the storyboard which proves that this is a good description.

Writing about Benedick and Beatrice

Look at this paragraph about Benedick. The notes around the paragraph show what job each part of it does.

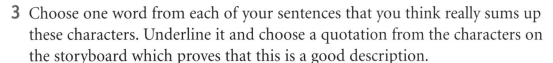

The **Point** of the paragraph – tells your reader what the paragraph is about.

The **Quotation** – evidence that proves your point.

The **Explanation** – explains how the evidence proves the point.

Benedick is very vain. He says to Beatrice:
'It is certain I am loved of all ladies, only you excepted.'
This suggests that Benedick thinks very highly of himself, especially as we only have his word for it. His use of the word 'certain' really emphasises his arrogance. It suggests that there can be no doubt that he is right.

A **colon** to introduce the evidence.

The evidence starts on a **new line** and is indented, like the first line of a paragraph. **Quotation marks** around the quotation. Notice that it doesn't translate the quotation into modern English.

A **comment on language** – picks out one word from the quote and shows how it proves the point.

Activity 7

You are going to write another two paragraphs about Beatrice and Benedick, using the paragraph on page 155 as an example. Follow steps 1–3 below.

Step 1: Look back at the three quotations you chose in Activity 6. Choose one that tells you something significant about one of these characters.

Step 2: Write your first paragraph explaining what the quotation shows about the character. Leave space around the paragraph for annotation. Check it against the example on page 155 to make sure you are using the same structure and punctuation.

Step 3: Using a different coloured pen, make annotations around your paragraph to show where you have used the seven features that are annotated in the example paragraph.

 Feedback

1 Swap your work with a partner. Check that your partner has annotated their work correctly and has included all the features shown in the example paragraph.
2 Discuss with your partner any changes they need to make to their paragraph.
3 Choose another quote and write your second paragraph, trying to include all seven of the features shown in the example paragraph on page 155. Annotate it to show these features.
4 Repeat this Feedback activity on the second paragraph.

Benedick – before and after

You are going to compare Benedick before and after he falls in love, and think about how Shakespeare creates comedy from this change.

Activity 8

In Act Two, Scene One, a great masked ball is being held at Leonato's house. Benedick and Don Pedro are talking when Beatrice approaches. Benedick asks to be sent on an errand, or mission, abroad so that he can get away from her. Read the following extract and answer the questions on page 157.

DON PEDRO	Look, here she comes.
BENEDICK	Will your grace command me any service to the world's end? I will go on the slightest errand now to the **Antipodes** that you can devise to send me on. I will fetch you a tooth-picker now from the furthest inch of Asia, bring you the length of **Prester John's** foot, fetch you a hair off the great **Cham's** beard, do you an embassage to the Pigmies, rather than hold three words' conference with this **harpy**. You have no employment for me?
DON PEDRO	None, but to desire your good company.
BENEDICK	O God sir, here's a **dish** I love not; I cannot endure my Lady Tongue.

Word bank

Antipodes the other side of the world
Prester John a priest believed to live in China
Cham the Emperor of China
harpy a mythical monster, half woman, half bird
dish a plate of food – and a pretty woman but Benedict means it as an insult

1 How many errands does Benedick suggest he should be sent on?

2 a What kinds of places and errands does Benedick suggest?
   b What point is he trying to make with these suggestions?
   c How is he making his point very clear?

3 What is Benedick suggesting about Beatrice when he calls her 'my Lady Tongue'?

4 What reaction is Benedick trying to get from Don Pedro?

5 Look again at the storyboard on pages 152–3. Why do you think Benedick is so insulting to Beatrice – and she to him?

Activity 9

In Act Two, Scene Three, Don Pedro, Leonato and Claudio discuss Beatrice's love for Benedick, knowing that he is listening. The following extract comes from the end of that scene. Benedick has already decided that he will love Beatrice. Read the extract and answer the questions to explore the ways in which Benedick has changed – and not changed.

BENEDICK	I did never think to marry. I must not seem proud. **Happy are they that hear their detractions and can put them to mending**. They say the lady is fair; 'tis a truth, I can bear them witness; and virtuous; so, I cannot reprove it; and wise, but for loving me. By my troth, **it is no addition to her wit, nor no great argument of her folly**, for I will be horribly in love with her.

Word bank

Happy are they … It is good to be able to put right the criticisms that people make of you
it is no … It does not make her more clever or more stupid

1 What three qualities does Benedick suddenly realise Beatrice has?

2 What word does Benedick use to describe the love he will have for Beatrice?

3 What does this word tell you about Benedick?

Progress check

This is an assessment of your understanding of:
- **a** the Beatrice and Benedick plot
- **b** how the audience might respond to the play
- **c** how Shakespeare appeals to his audience
- **d** how to write about Shakespeare.

You are going to compare two quotations from Beatrice, taken from different points in the play.
First, in Act One, Scene One, she says: 'I had rather hear my dog bark at a crow than a man swear he loves me.'
Later, in Act Four, Scene One, she says to Benedick: 'I love you with so much of my heart that none is left to protest.'
Use these quotations to write two paragraphs about the character of Beatrice.

How do I write the paragraphs?
Try to:
- use the **P**oint-**Q**uotation-**E**xplanation structure
- comment on Shakespeare's choice of language
- use the correct punctuation and layout.

Look back at page 155 if you need a reminder of how to write this kind of paragraph.

What do I write about?
In the first paragraph, explain:
- what the audience's first impressions of Beatrice might be.

In the second paragraph, explain:
- how and why Beatrice has changed
- what effect this might have on the audience
- how Shakespeare is appealing to his audience.

When you have written your two paragraphs, check that you have achieved as many of the bullet-pointed criteria above as you can.

Hero and Claudio, Don John and the Watch

You are now going to look at the other plots which, together with the story of Beatrice and Benedick, make up the whole play of *Much Ado About Nothing*. Opposite are the characters you need to meet.

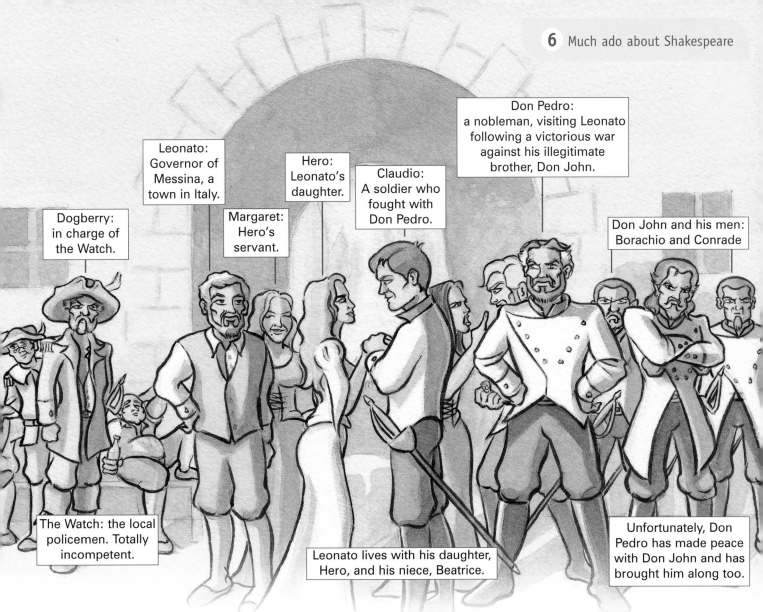

Dogberry: in charge of the Watch.

Leonato: Governor of Messina, a town in Italy.

Margaret: Hero's servant.

Hero: Leonato's daughter.

Claudio: A soldier who fought with Don Pedro.

Don Pedro: a nobleman, visiting Leonato following a victorious war against his illegitimate brother, Don John.

Don John and his men: Borachio and Conrade

The Watch: the local policemen. Totally incompetent.

Leonato lives with his daughter, Hero, and his niece, Beatrice.

Unfortunately, Don Pedro has made peace with Don John and has brought him along too.

Activity 10

Look carefully at the characters above. You are going to make some predictions about how they will behave in the story based on their appearance, attitude to other characters and stance. Answer the questions and give a short explanation, commenting on the clues that helped you.

1 Who do you think is a 'good' character?

2 Who do you think is a 'bad' character?

3 Which characters will add comedy to the play?

4 Which characters will add excitement and action to the play?

When you have read the storyboard on pages 160–62, check your predictions to see if you were right.

The Story of Hero and Claudio, Don John and the Watch

① In mine eye she is the sweetest lady that ever I looked on.

While Beatrice and Benedick bicker constantly, Claudio falls instantly in love with Leonato's daughter, Hero. He tells Don Pedro.

② … though I cannot be said to be a flattering honest man, it must not be denied but I am a plain-dealing villain.

Don John is planning to upset everything and show everyone that he is proud to be evil.

③ I will assume thy part in some disguise, And tell fair Hero I am Claudio, And in her bosom I'll unclasp my heart, …

To celebrate his guests' visit, Leonato gives a ball. All the guests wear masks, which allows some confusion to be created. Claudio is reluctant to approach Hero, so Don Pedro says he will pretend to be Claudio and woo Hero on his behalf.

④ 'Tis certain so; the prince woos for himself.

Signor, you are very near my brother in his love. He is enamoured on Hero; I pray you dissuade him from her; she is no equal for his birth.

Don John pretends to Claudio that he thinks he is talking to Benedick. It's all part of his plot to spoil everyone's happiness. He tries to make Claudio think Don Pedro wants Hero for himself. Claudio believes him.

⑤ Lady, as you are mine, I am yours.

Here Claudio, I have wooed in thy name, and fair Hero is won … name the day of marriage, and God give thee joy.

Don Pedro, though, has good news: Hero has agreed to marry Claudio. He tells Claudio, who now declares his love for Hero.

⑥ Go but with me tonight, you shall see her chamber-window entered, even the night before her wedding-day. If you love her then, tomorrow wed her; but it would better fit your honour to change your mind.

To pass the time before their marriage, Claudio and Hero plot to trick Beatrice and Benedick into loving each other. However, their own happiness is in grave danger from Don John's plotting. Don John tells Claudio that Hero is having an affair – and advises Claudio to call off the marriage.

Claudio and Don Pedro see Hero helping a man climb through her bedroom window. They do not realise that the woman is not Hero; it is her servant, Margaret, dressed as Hero; and the man is Borachio, her boyfriend, and one of Don John's men.

Borachio cannot resist boasting of his cleverness to his friend, Conrade. However, they are overheard by the Watch, who arrest them.

And thought they Margaret was Hero?

I have tonight wooed Margaret, the Lady Hero's gentlewoman …

We charge you, in the Prince's name, stand!

There, Leonato, take her back again, Give not this rotten orange to your friend – She's but the sign and semblance of her honour.

The news that it was all a plot by Don John does not arrive in time to stop Claudio. At the wedding, in front of the Friar and all their friends, Claudio tells Hero's father, Leonato, that he does not want his daughter – she is not the honourable woman she once seemed. Hero faints in horror.

O she is fallen Into a pit of ink, that the wide sea Hath drops too few to wash her clean again.

Beatrice tries to comfort Hero but Leonato is distraught and wishes that Hero would die because her reputation is ruined forever.

Let her awhile be secretly kept in, And publish it that she is dead indeed.

The Friar is unsure whether the accusations are true and makes a suggestion. If everyone thinks Hero has died of shame, they will forgive her more easily and it will give Leonato some time to find out the truth.

⑫

… they have committed false report; moreover they have spoken untruths; secondarily, they are slanders; sixth and lastly, they have belied a lady; thirdly, they have verified unjust things; and to conclude, they are lying knaves.

The Watch arrest Conrade and Borachio and bring them to Leonato. Dogberry explains their crimes in a lot of detail, creating a lot of confusion.

⑬

Choose your revenge …

I have deceived even your very eyes.

Borachio confesses that he and Don John faked Hero's crime. Claudio is horrified at the consequences of his mistake. He asks Leonato for forgiveness and a punishment.

⑭

And since you could not be my son-in-law, Be yet my nephew. My brother hath a daughter, … Give her the right you should have given her cousin, And so dies my revenge.

Instead of taking revenge, Leonato asks that he marry a cousin of Hero's.

⑮

She died my lord, but whiles her slander lived.

The former Hero! Hero that is dead!

At the church, Hero's cousin is revealed. It is Hero herself, to everyone's amazement and delight. Leonato explains that she was only dead while the lies about her were alive.

⑯

Let's have a dance 'ere we are married, that we may lighten our own hearts and our wives' heels.

Don John is caught when he tries to run away. Hero and Claudio – and Beatrice and Benedick – are married. They dance in celebration.

Performing the story

Now that you have looked at the story of Hero and Claudio, Don John and the Watch, you are going to write a script of the story for another group to perform. You will need to include stage directions to indicate how you want the characters to speak, look and move. You will assess your script using the other group's performance of it to help you.

Activity 11

1 Working in a group, choose **either** the first eight frames **or** the last eight frames of the storyboard on pages 160–62. For each frame, write down one word from each character which you feel really sums up what they are saying. For example, from Frame 1, you are looking for one word that sums up how Claudio feels about Hero. You might choose *sweetest*.

2 Add some stage directions to help the performers. Think about the characters' movements, facial expressions, how they should say their word. Look at this example to help you:

Scene 1
Claudio kneels in front of Hero, staring up at her.
Claudio (adoringly): Sweetest!

3 When you have finished writing your script, swap with another group and rehearse your performance. Try to follow their script and stage directions as closely as possible. You will be able to have your script when you perform, but try to remember as many words and actions as you can.

 Feedback

You are going to assess your script. Remember, you are not assessing how well the other group performed. Use the following criteria.
- Does the script tell the same story as the storyboard?
- Did the performance suggested by your stage directions help you to understand the characters and the story?

After the performance, complete the following sentences to help you identify what worked well and how you could use this to improve your script.
- The most successful point in the script was …
- What made it really successful was …
- The least successful point in the script was …
- We could make it more successful by …

Keep a record of your comments to help you improve your next performance later in the unit.

Explaining characters – Hero and Claudio

You are going to look at the roles of Hero and Claudio in the play. Use the storyboard on pages 160–62 to help you answer the following questions.

Activity 12

1 Write down **five** things that Claudio does or has done to him. For each one, write down what it suggests about his character. For example:
   Claudio falls in love with Hero before she has even said a word to him. This suggests that he is young and is easily impressed by beauty.

2 **a** Write down what Hero says and does, and what happens to her. Discuss with a partner how you would react in the same situations. What does this suggest about her character?
   b Now look back to the Beatrice and Benedick storyboard on pages 152–3. What does Hero do in that part of the play? Does this change or add to your view of Hero's character?

Soliloquy

In a film, we see a face and hear their thoughts as a *voice over*. For obvious reasons, Shakespeare couldn't use this technique. Instead, he used **soliloquies** where a character, usually alone on stage, expresses their thoughts aloud to the audience. A soliloquy can help to create:

- characterisation – explains how the character feels
- plot development – explains what he or she intends to do next, and why
- comic dramatic irony – makes the audience laugh because they know more than the character at this point
- suspense dramatic irony – makes the audience tense because the character is unaware of the danger in a situation.

When Claudio is told by Don John that Don Pedro is wooing Hero for himself, Claudio believes him. Claudio expresses his reaction in a soliloquy.

CLAUDIO	'Tis certain so; the Prince woos for himself.
	Friendship is constant in all other things
	Save in the office and affairs of love.
	Therefore all hearts in love use their own tongues.
5	Let every eye negotiate for itself,
	And trust no agent; for beauty is a witch
	Against whose charms **faith** melteth into **blood**.
	This is an accident of hourly proof,
	Which I mistrusted not. Farewell therefore Hero.

Word bank

faith loyalty
blood passion
This is an … this happens all the time

Activity 13

1 Write a modern English version of what Claudio is saying here.

2 Claudio uses a metaphor to describe beauty. He says it is 'a witch'. What is he suggesting?

3 Look at the list of the effects a soliloquy can create. Which of these four effects do you think this soliloquy has? Write a paragraph explaining the effect(s) you have chosen. Use a quotation as evidence and try to explain how this tells us about the effect you have identified. You can follow this **P**oint-**Q**uotation-**E**xplanation structure to help you:

Point – the soliloquy tells us about the character of Claudio
Quotation – he says …
Explanation – this suggests that …

The villain

The following activities will explore the role of the villain in *Much Ado About Nothing*. At the start of the play, Don John has been defeated in war by his brother Don Pedro. He makes it clear in Act One, Scene Three what he is like and the kind of things we will see him do. He says:

> **DON JOHN** … though I cannot be said to be a flattering honest man, it must not be denied but I am a plain-dealing villain. I am trusted with a **muzzle** and **enfranchised with a clog**; therefore **I have decreed not to sing in my cage**. If I had my mouth, I would bite; if I had my liberty, I would do my liking. In the meantime, let me be that I am …
>
> 5

Word bank
muzzle kind of mask fitted to an animal's jaws to stop it biting
enfranchised … wearing a ball and chain to restrict a prisoner's movements
I have decreed … I will not take my punishment happily

Activity 14

1 Make a list of villains from books, films or plays you know.

2 Looking at your list, write down the qualities you think a villain should have.

3 What villainous qualities can you find in the short speech by Don John?

4 How does this speech hint at what will happen later in the play? Why do you think Shakespeare gave Don John this speech so early in the play?

5 What do the words 'muzzle' and 'clog' suggest about how Don John feels he is being treated after his defeat?

6 How could an audience be made to feel sorry for Don John? Write some suggestions for the actor playing Don John so he can get some sympathy from the audience. Think about:
- how he should speak some of the lines   • his facial expression
- how he should stand.

✓ Progress check

You are being assessed on your understanding of:

- the Hero and Claudio plot
- the character of Don John
- the effect of soliloquices
- the play in performance.

You are going to write a soliloquy in modern English for Don John, to be spoken at the end of the play. Before you begin to write, you need to decide:

a what Don John's feelings would be at this point

b what effect you want your soliloquy to have on the audience – remind yourself of the work you did on soliloquies on page 164

c what stage directions you could give the actor playing Don John to achieve this effect.

Write about ten lines. Your aims are to show:

- how Don John feels about his failure to prevent Hero and Claudio's marriage
- what the character of Don John is like.

When you have written your soliloquy, annotate your work to show where you have achieved the two aims above. Then write four or five sentences explaining what effect this soliloquy should have on the audience and how the words you have chosen will create that effect.

Performance

You have already looked at a short extract from Act Two, Scene Three to explore how Benedick changes during the play. You are now going to look at a series of extracts from that scene and prepare a performance of them.

Exploring how to turn script into action

Activity 15

Working with a partner, discuss and write down your answers to the questions on each extract.

1 At the beginning of the scene, Benedick is in Leonato's orchard, thinking aloud about Claudio. Claudio used to laugh at men who fell in love, and now he has fallen in love himself. Benedick is laughing at him.

> **BENEDICK** I do much wonder that one man, seeing how much another man is a fool when he dedicates his behaviours to love, will, after he hath laughed at such shallow follies in others, become the argument of his own scorn by falling in love; and such a man is Claudio.

How should Benedick speak these lines? Is he angry or sad that his friend has changed? Or perhaps Benedick is pleased with himself for being less foolish than Claudio?

2 Benedick sees Don Pedro, Leonato and Claudio coming and hides.

> **BENEDICK**   I will hide me in the arbour.

This is the only clue Shakespeare gives us for the staging of this scene. How would you arrange this on stage? An arbour is a group of trees – but you might want to use a different device – perhaps some bushes or a hedge. Remember that the audience must be able to see and hear all the characters – and believe that Benedick thinks he is well hidden.

3 As his friends talk, Benedick listens. They edge closer to be sure that he can hear them.

DON PEDRO	Come hither Leonato. What was it you told me of today, that your niece Beatrice was in love with Signor Benedick?
CLAUDIO	[*aside*] O ay, stalk on. **Stalk on; the fowl sits**. – I did never think that lady would have loved any man.
LEONATO	No nor I neither; but most wonderful that she should dote so on Signor Benedick, whom she hath in all outward behaviour seemed ever to abhor.
BENEDICK	[*aside*] Is't possible? **Sits the wind in that corner?**
LEONATO	By my troth my lord, I cannot tell what to think of it; but that she loves him with an enraged affection …

> **Word bank**
>
> **stalk on; the fowl sits**
> Claudio is using the language of hunting. He means 'Get nearer, Benedick is ready to be caught.'
> **Sits the wind …**
> Is that the way the wind's blowing? Is that the way it is?

An **aside** is a line spoken by a character which is not meant to be heard by some or all of the other characters on the stage. The two asides in this extract are used in different ways. Benedick's aside allows him to express his thoughts to the audience – he can't quite believe his ears. Claudio's aside indicates that this is to be heard by Leonato and Don Pedro – but not by Benedick.

How could the actor playing Benedick deliver his aside to show his reaction to the news?

How could the actor playing Claudio deliver his aside so that the audience knows only Don Pedro and Leonato can hear it – and then the rest of that line ('I did never think that lady would have loved any man') so that the audience knows that Benedick is meant to hear it?

4 Leonato says he has heard that Beatrice keeps trying to write a love letter to Benedick.

> **LEONATO** This says she now when she is beginning to write to him; for she'll be up twenty times a night, and there will she sit in her **smock** till she have writ a sheet of paper – my daughter tells us all.
>
> **CLAUDIO** Now you talk of a sheet of paper, I remember a pretty jest your daughter told us of.
>
> **LEONATO** O, when she had writ it and was reading it over, she found Benedick and Beatrice **between the sheet**?

Word bank

smock nightclothes
between the sheet a pun or double meaning: a sheet of paper – or bed sheets
conference was sadly borne the news was spoken seriously
have their full bent are extreme
requited returned

How does Leonato show his friends and the audience that he is making a pun? How should Claudio and Don Pedro react? How does Benedick react in his hiding place?

5 Claudio goes even further to persuade Benedick that Beatrice truly loves him.

> **CLAUDIO** ... down upon her knees she falls, weeps, sobs, beats her heart, tears her hair, prays, curses – 'O sweet Benedick! God give me patience!'

How should Claudio speak these lines? Is their purpose to convince Benedick? Or to make the audience laugh?

6 Claudio, Leonato and Don Pedro leave. Benedick has been convinced.

> **BENEDICK** This can be no trick. The **conference was sadly borne**. They have the truth of this from Hero. They seem to pity the lady. It seems her affections **have their full bent**. Love me? Why, it must be **requited**.

How can the actor show Benedick realising what this means? Should he realise slowly? How could his reactions change and develop?

Now look back to the first extract from this scene, where Benedick laughed at the change in Claudio when he fell in love. It is ironic that Benedick has done exactly the same thing that he complained about Claudio doing. How could the actor playing Benedick help the audience notice this irony?

Preparing your performance

Activity 16

You are now going to prepare a complete performance of all these extracts from Act Two, Scene Three. Your performance will be assessed by another group. You will be assessed on:

- your understanding of the plot and characters in the scene
- how your voice, actions and facial expressions add comedy to the scene.

Follow steps 1–5 below.

Step 1

Write two short character guides: one for Benedick, the other for Leonato, Don Pedro and Claudio, explaining how they have come to be in this situation.

Step 2

In your group, compare your answers to the questions in Activity 15 and decide how you will perform the scene. You will need to add stage directions. Write down:

- how each line should be spoken
- what actions and facial expressions will help explain their meaning – and perhaps make the audience laugh.

Step 3

What other actions could you add to create comedy? For example, what if Benedick peeps out from his hiding place and is almost seen? Add these stage directions to your notes.

Step 4

Decide who will play which part. Rehearse the scene, using the comments you recorded as part of the Feedback on page 163 to set a target for your script.

Step 5

Perform the scene to another group. You can use your script, but try to remember as many words and actions as you can.

 Feedback

In your group, you are going to assess another group's performance by answering the following questions.

- Did the performance tell the story clearly?
- Did the characters match your understanding of the story?
- Was the performance funny?
- Was the comedy created using a combination of voice, facial expression and actions?

Comparing plots

In *Much Ado About Nothing* (and in all plays, novels, and films), some ideas and events come up again and again in different ways. You are going to compare the different plots of *Much Ado* and look at how they explore the same ideas or themes.

Activity 17

1 To help you compare the two plots of Beatrice and Benedick, and Hero and Claudio, complete the table below.

Hero and Claudio	*Beatrice and Benedick*
Hero and Claudio fall in _____ at first sight.	Beatrice and Benedick eventually admit that they _____ each other.
Don John and his men _____ Claudio into believing that Hero has been unfaithful to him.	Hero and Claudio _____ Beatrice and Benedick into believing that they love each other.
Don John admits to the audience that he is a villain. He may be a villain but at least he's _____. Claudio believes that Hero could be unfaithful. He says he loves her, but perhaps he is not being _____ with himself.	Like Beatrice, Benedick falls in love very easily. Perhaps he loved Beatrice all along but was not being _____ with himself.
At the end of the play, we see the _____ of Hero and Claudio.	At the end of the play, we see the _____ of Beatrice and Benedick.

2 Look at the words you used to fill the gaps. What ideas or themes are explored throughout *Much Ado About Nothing*?

Exploring themes

These ideas are also known as the **themes** of the play. The two plots have similar themes, but they are explored in different ways.

Activity 18

1 Look again at the different stages of the story in the table. Which do you think Shakespeare intended to make his audience laugh, and which did he use to create suspense?

2 The reasons for audience appeal are listed again below. Match the themes of *Much Ado* against the type of appeal they would have to an audience.
  • It will make the audience forget about the real world.
  • It will make the audience think about the world we live in.
  • It will make the audience think about their own lives and what is important.
  • It will appeal to the audience's feelings and emotions.

3 You are going to explore further how Shakespeare might be trying to make his audience think about their lives and what is important. Look at these scenes from *Much Ado*. For each one, write a sentence explaining:
  a what point in the play it is taken from
  b the warnings or advice Shakespeare may be giving us about our attitudes and feelings and their consequences.

Assessment task

Understanding Much Ado About Nothing

In this task you are going to:

- read two short extracts from *Much Ado About Nothing*
- answer some questions to help you understand and analyse these extracts
- use the skills and understanding you have gained during the unit to help you complete an extended written task on the extracts.

You will be assessed on:

- your understanding of the story of the play and where these extracts fit in to it
- your knowledge of the characters in the play and their different attitudes to marriage
- your awareness of how the actors could show these different attitudes through their performance
- your ability to support and develop your ideas using quotations.

Text A – from Act Two, Scene One

Leonato and his brother, Antonio, mistakenly think that Don Pedro is going to propose to Hero. They are checking that she will give the right answer. Beatrice, however, is quite clear that she does not want to marry anyone.

ANTONIO	[*To Hero*] Well niece, I trust you will be ruled by your father.
BEATRICE	Yes faith, it is my cousin's duty to make curtsy and say, 'Father, as it please you'. But yet for all that, cousin, let him be a handsome fellow, or else make another curtsy and say, 'Father, as it please me'.
LEONATO	Well, niece, I hope to see you one day fitted with a husband.
BEATRICE	Not till God make men of some other metal than earth. Would it not grieve a woman to be overmastered with a piece of valiant dust? To make an account of her life to a clod of wayward **marl**? No, uncle, I'll none. **Adam's sons are my brethren, and truly I hold it a sin to match in my kindred.**
LEONATO	[*To Hero*] Daughter, remember what I told you: if the Prince do **solicit you in that kind**, you know your answer.

Word bank

marl earth or soil. God made man from the earth; Beatrice will not marry someone made of dirt!
Adam's sons are … all men are my brothers and it's a sin to marry one of your own family
solicit you in that kind ask you to marry him

1 Look at what Leonato and Antonio say to Hero. What does it suggest about the men and their attitude to marriage?

2 Shakespeare has given Hero no lines here. What does this suggest about her response to Leonato and Antonio and their attitude to marriage?

3 Beatrice reminds Hero about her duty. But what advice does she give her?

4 What is Beatrice's view of men and marriage?

5 How would an audience react to Beatrice and Hero's very different personalities and attitudes to marriage? Would everyone in the audience have the same reaction?

Text B – from Act Four, Scene One

It is the wedding of Claudio and Hero; but Don John has tricked Claudio into thinking that Hero has been unfaithful to him. Claudio is going to refuse to marry her.

FRIAR	You come hither, my lord, to marry this lady?
CLAUDIO	No.
LEONATO	To be married to her. Friar, you come to marry her.
FRIAR	Lady, you come hither to be married to this Count.
HERO	I do.
FRIAR	If either of you know any inward impediment why you should not be conjoined, charge you on your souls, to utter it.
CLAUDIO	Know you any, Hero?
HERO	None my lord.
FRIAR	Know you any, Count?
LEONATO	I dare make his answer, None.
CLAUDIO	O what men dare do! What men may do! What men daily do, not knowing what they do!
BENEDICK	How now, interjections? Why then, some be of laughing, as, ah, ha, he!
CLAUDIO	Stand thee by, Friar. Father, by your leave – Will you with free and unconstrained soul. Give me this maid your daughter?
LEONATO	As freely, son, as God did give her me.
CLAUDIO	And what have I to give you back, whose worth May **counterpoise** this rich and precious gift?
DON PEDRO	Nothing, unless you **render her** again.
CLAUDIO	Sweet Prince, you **learn me noble thankfulness**. There Leonato, take her back again, Give not this rotten orange to your friend – She's but the sign and semblance of her honour.

Word bank

counterpoise balance
render her give her back
learn me noble thankfulness teach me good manners or gratitude

1 When does Claudio first suggest he does not want to marry Hero?

2 How do Leonato and Benedick excuse Claudio's strange behaviour?

3 Make a list of all the things Claudio calls Hero in this extract. Which is the odd one out – and why?

4 What does this extract suggest about Claudio's attitude to love and marriage?

5 Shakespeare makes Claudio wait until the wedding to announce that he will not marry Hero. What is the effect of this on:
   a the plot
   b the other characters
   c the audience?

Writing about Text A and Text B

You are now going to write a longer answer to this question: **What impressions might an audience get of these characters' attitudes to marriage?**
Follow steps 1–7 below to organise your writing.

Step 1
Identify the key words in the question you are going to answer.

Step 2
Gather all the different attitudes to marriage in these extracts. Make a note of characters who hold similar opinions – and characters whose opinions are very different.

Step 3
For each of these opinions, find a quotation as evidence. This evidence will become the central part of each paragraph you write.

Step 4
Write a short introduction: introduce the question (but don't repeat it), explaining what these two extracts have got to do with marriage.

Step 5
Using your quotations, write four or five paragraphs to explain the characters' different attitudes to marriage. Each paragraph should have:
- a clear point
- a relevant quotation
- an explanation of how the actors could show their character's attitude to the audience
- a comment on language exploring the effect Shakespeare intended in his choice of words.

Look back at the work you did on **P**oint-**Q**uotation-**E**xplanation-**C**omment on page 155, if you need to.

Step 6
Write a conclusion that answers the question. Make sure it includes the question's key words.

Step 7
Look carefully over your work and annotate it to show where it achieves the four assessment criteria on page 172. Make any changes you need to improve your work.

Heinemann Educational Publishers
Halley Court, Jordan Hill, Oxford OX2 8EJ
Part of Harcourt Education

Heinemann is the registered trademark of Harcourt Education Limited

© Harcourt Education Limited, 2005

First published 2005

10 09 08 07 06 05
10 9 8 7 6 5 4 3 2 1

British Library Cataloguing in Publication Data is available from the British Library on request.

10-digit ISBN: 0 435 22770 X
13-digit ISBN: 978 0 435227 70 8

Cover design by Wooden Ark Studio   Designed by Wooden Ark Studio   Printed By Bath Colour Books
Cover photo: © Getty   Produced by Kamae Design

Original illustrations © Harcourt Education Limited, 2005

Illustrated by **Johanna Boccardo:** pp120, 131; **Chris Brown:** pp50, 54–55, 105, 106–107, 108–109, 110–111, 112; **Mark Draisey:** p125; **Alice Englander:** pp90, 92–93; **Peter Greenwood:** pp66, 67, 68, 118; **Phil Healey:** pp7, 39, 127; **Karin Littlewood:** p47 **Sean Longcroft:** pp146–147; **Georgina McBain:** p43; **Andrew Morris:** pp49, 72, 151, 152, 153, 155, 157, 159, 160, 161, 162, 165, 168, 171, 173

Photos: p6 Granada TV; p12L John Birdsall Social Issue Photography; pp12**R**, 23, 31, 33, 44, 45, 58, 70, 75**B1**, 76**B1**, 80, 83, 84, 97**T**, 97**B**, 97**R**, 98, 99, 103, 115, 138, 139, 143**T2**, 143**B2** Corbis; p22 FLPA/Mitsuaki Iwago/Minden Pictures; p28 Copyright © Stockport County; p30 Reuters/Toby Melville; p36 Alamy; pp41, 73, Rex Features; p62 Photodisc; p65 Ardea; p66 Harcourt Education Ltd/Digital Vision; pp70**M**, 133, 143**T1**, 143**B1** Getty Images;pp75**T2**, 76**T2** Jim West/Alamy; pp 75**T1**, 76**T1**, pp77, 129 Harcourt Education Ltd/Photodisc; p122 Harcourt Education Ltd; p129 Image Source Spirit/Alamy; p129**M** Harcourt Education Ltd/Tudor Photography

Acknowledgements

Every effort has been made to contact copyright holders of material reproduced in this book. Any omissions will be rectified in subsequent printings if notice is given to the publishers.

Cover of *PRIMA* magazine, January 2005. Copyright © National Magazine Company/PRIMA. Reprinted with permission; cover of *Car* magazine, January 2005. Copyright © EMAP. Reprinted with permission of EMAP Automotive Ltd; cover and contents of *Q* magazine, January 2005. Copyright © EMAP. Reprinted with permission; cover of *Powerstation* magazine, issue 106. Copyright © Highbury Entertainment Ltd. Reprinted with permission; cover of *Sugar* magazine, October 2004. Copyright © Hachette Filipacchi (UK) Ltd. Reprinted with permission; *BBC Teens* webpage from *BBC Teens* website. Copyright © BBC. Reprinted with permission of the *BBC Teens* website; 'Dead Leaves' advertisement. Copyright © Manga Entertainment Ltd (www.manga.co.uk). Reprinted with permission of Manga Entertainment Ltd; 'Welcome to the Stockport County FC Study Centre' taken from a Stockport Study Centre flyer. Reprinted with permission of the Stockport Study Centre; article 'Beagle puppies stolen from hunt kennels', 28th October 2004, and article 'Hunt set for biggest day in its history', 22nd December 2003, from www.countryside-alliance.org. Reprinted with permission of The Countryside Alliance; 'Pets and the Urban Fox' from www.nfws.org.uk. Reprinted with permission; article 'League Deplores hunt harassment in Brighton', 28th September 2004, from www.league.uk.com. Reprinted with permission; article 'Whizz Kid' by Mike Bradley, *Stockport Times East*, Thursday 30th September 2004. Reprinted with permission; article '"Off" night for Bury!' *Bury Times*, Friday 1st October 2004. Reprinted with permission; article '£1.8bn – the cost of Christmas toys', Tuesday 9th November 2004, from www.manchesteronline.co.uk; extract from 'Should junk food ads be banned?' by Ray Dunne, Wednesday 7th April 2004. Reprinted with kind permission of the BBC, Dr David Ashton, and Professor Gerard Hastings; 'Progress' by Hilaire Belloc, from *Complete Verse*, published by Pimlico. Reprinted by permission of The Estate of Hilaire Belloc, c/o PFD © Estate of Hilaire Belloc 1970; 'Cinquain' by Valerie Bloom, from *The Works*, edited by Paul Cookson, published by Macmillan Children's Books. Copyright © 2000 Valerie Bloom. Reprinted by permission of Valerie Bloom c/o Eddison Pearson Ltd; 'The Vixen' by John Clare, 1793–1865; extract from *Face* by Benjamin Zephaniah, published by Bloomsbury. Copyright © Benjamin Zephaniah. Reprinted with permission of the publishers; extracts from *Mortal Engines* by Philip Reeve. Copyright © Philip Reeve 2001, published by Scholastic Children's Books. All rights reserved. Reproduced by permission of Scholastic Ltd; extracts from *The Curious Incident of The Dog In The Night-Time* by Mark Haddon, published by David Fickling/Red Fox. Reprinted by permission of The Random House Group Ltd; 'Mother' by Stephen Elboz, from *The Young Oxford Book of Supernatural Stories*, edited by Dennis Pepper, published by Oxford University Press 1996. Copyright © Stephen Elboz, 1996. Reprinted with the kind permission of the author; extracts from *Ruby Tanya* by Robert Swindells, published by Doubleday. Reprinted with permission of the Random House Group Ltd; 'Red Alert' and 'Gorillas' from www.iucn.org, The World Conservation Union; extract from 'Hold the pocket money!' by Katherine Sheehy, Newswise www.dialogueworks.co.uk; extract from 'How happy children are' from www.unicef.org.uk. Copyright © UNICEF. Reprinted with permission; extract from 'Employers take notice – success is happiness; not money', from the Learning & Skills Council www.lsc.gov.uk; extract about pilot study by the New Economics foundation, from NEF New Economics Foundation. Reprinted with permission; 'Bullying in schools' adapted from DfES report 'Tackling Bullying' 2003 © Crown Copyright; extract from 'Ashputtel, or The Mother's Ghost' by Angela Carter, from *The Virago Book of Ghost Stories*, first published by Virago 1987. Copyright © 1987 Angela Carter. Reproduced by permission of the author c/o Rogers Coleridge & White Ltd, 20 Powis Mews, London W11 1JN; 'The Photograph' by Sefi Atta. Copyright © Sefi Atta. Reprinted with the kind permission of the author; 'A Drink of Water' by Samuel Selvon. Reprinted with the kind permission of Althea Selvon; 'A Morning Swim' by Madhulika Liddle. Copyright © Madhulika Liddle. Reprinted with the kind permission of the author; extract from *Zlata's Diary: A Child's Life in Sarajevo* by Zlata Filipovic, translated by Christina Pribichevich-Zoric, published by Viking 1994. First published in France as 'Le Journal de Zlata' by Fixot et éditions Robert Laffont 1993. Copyright © Fixot et éditions Robert Laffont. Reprinted with permission of Penguin Books Ltd; extracts from *Diary Of A Teenage Health Freak* by Aidan Macfarlane and Ann McPherson, published by OUP 2002. Copyright © Aidan Macfarlane and Ann McPherson 1987, 1996, 2002. Reprinted by permission of Oxford University Press; extract from 'The Lever Faberge Family Report 2004: Parenting Under The Microscope'. Reprinted with permission of Blue Rubicon; article 'Why I Love Fat Babies' by Glenn Waldron, The Guardian, 27th January 2004. Copyright © Glenn Waldron. Reprinted with the kind permission of the author; 'Don't Be Scared of Those Sharks' by David Slack, from www.speeches.com. Reprinted with permission.